Towards Self-governing Schools

Dick Atkinson

Published by the IEA Education and Training Unit, 1997

First published in October 1997 by
The Institute of Economic Affairs
2 Lord North Street
Westminster
London SW1P 3LB

© IEA 1997

IEA Studies in Education No. 4
All rights reserved

ISBN 0-255 36408-3

Many IEA publications are translated into languages other than English or are reprinted. Permission to translate or to reprint should be sought from the General Director at the address above.

Printed in Great Britain by
Hartington Fine Arts Limited, Lancing, West Sussex
Set in Century Schoolbook and Bookman Old Style

Contents

	Foreword *Dr James Tooley*	5
	The Author	8
	Acknowledgements	8
	Executive Summary	11
	The Third Way	11
	School Autonomy	12
1	**Introduction**	18
2	**The Rationale for Moving to Self-Government**	24
	Self-Reliance and the Modern Business Organisation	24
	The Two Cultures and Languages of Dependence and Autonomy	27
3	**Changing Rôles in Self-Government**	34
	Governors	34
	Headteachers	35
	Independent Suppliers of Educational Services	36
	LEAs and Diminishing Education Budgets	38
	Towards a National Funding Formula	41
	The First Steps towards Clustering – Schools Providing Services for Themselves	41
	Administration and Cluster Development	46
	Co-operation and Clusters	48
	A Possible Future – Schools and Clusters as Family Centres for their Neighbourhood	50
	Educational Enterprises	52
	Self-Government and Community Education and Development	53

4	**Choice and Diversity and the Virtues of Self-Government**	55
	Variety Is the Spice of Life	55
	Choice, Diversity and Demand	60
	Does the LEA Have a Function?	64
	The Funding of Local Authorities	69
5	**New LEA, New Town Hall**	71
6	**Conclusion and Recommendations**	78
	Appendix	83

Figures

1. Models of Management in Industrial and Post-Industrial Society	26
2. The Collectivist Model	32
3. The Individualist Model	32
4. The Outcome of the Two-Tier System	33
5. The Radical Alternative	33
6. Percentage of Schools Sharing Different Facilities	43
7. A Typical Cluster Pyramid	43
8. The Cluster Model	45
9. The Maypole System	45
10. Town Hall Structure	75
References/Bibliography	86
Summary	*Back Cover*

Foreword

In the autumn of 1997, the government announced that Her Majesty's Chief Inspector of Schools, Chris Woodhead, no longer trusted the London Borough of Hackney to run its education service. This was important news: parents and children in that borough would no longer have to suffer under incompetent and politicised management, with education being allowed 'to drift' under its 'paralysing' influence (*Times Educational Supplement*, 26 September 1997). In all the discussion that followed this announcement in the press, on radio and on television, no-one raised the question which troubles Dr Dick Atkinson. While everyone else sought possible mechanisms for rescuing the failing Local Education Authority (LEA), no-one raised the issue of whether local government involvement in education is part of the problem, rather than a necessary part of any solution.

In this challenging paper, Dr Atkinson raises the question: why do we need local education authorities at all? Finding reasons lacking, he puts forward a proposal for all schools to be *self-governing*. He points out that further and higher education do not need LEA involvement, that financial management is best accomplished by schools themselves, and that outside agencies are now available to offer quality services in almost every area of school life, from curriculum support, through careers services, to the supply of temporary teaching staff. Where such opportunities are not available, this is 'a direct consequence of the lingering LEA monopoly' (p. 65). If LEAs were to be abolished now, he points out, considerably more funds would be available for the classroom, schools could become accountable to their communities and customers they serve rather than to 'remote bureaucrats', and schools would cease to be part of the 'dependency culture'. Instead, unencumbered by the often-negative influence of the local authorities, schools would embrace the opportunities to raise educational standards, to promote innovation, and improve access.

Atkinson's alternative to local-government control is for schools to link together voluntarily, creating clusters. It is not the only possible way forward, of course; and if schools truly were to be made self-governing then this would be one of the myriad possibilities that could emerge, from self-standing schools, proud of their independent traditions, to chains of for-profit schools administered from a lean, central quality control office.

Dick Atkinson writes with a passion and seriousness inspired by his own personal involvement in education. He is perhaps best known for his work in Birmingham, where he established St Paul's Community School, for 'at risk' young people who have been excluded from mainstream schools. This school has recently 'opted in' to grant-maintained status – that is, has become government funded, but outside of any local education authority control. Atkinson fears what might happen if the Labour government were to force such schools into the 'one-size-fits-all' of local government control. His writing is a challenge to anyone who would seek to impose such an end on schools which have flourished and excelled outside of that tutelage.

In the end, he does not bite the bullet and propose the abolition of town hall control of schools; he stops short and suggests some 'steering' role for them. Some readers may decide that here Dick Atkinson is being too generous – although they would go along with his proposal that any remaining LEA rump should definitely not have any control over schools' budgets. The problem – for this reader at least – is that local education authorities have always had such a 'steering' role, and its positive educational impact has not been obvious – as indeed pointed out decisively by Atkinson in this monograph. It is arguable that it is precisely such a 'steering' role that has led to the politicisation of schooling, with all its negative impact on standards and equality of opportunity. The leaner, more localised LEA may not suffer such consequences, particularly if its budget and potential for power are severely curtailed as Atkinson suggests; however, vested political interests can have a way of circumventing such restrictions. But most importantly, if schools are self-governing and accountable to the communities they serve and to their consumers, it is not clear why the 'steering' function cannot emerge from below, as it were. What more of value can local politicians add? How would they avoid the unhelpful party political wrangling which has made education such a political 'football' in England and Wales?

In any case, whatever differences may emerge in the details of the proposal, Dr Atkinson's work is an important contribution to a timely debate. Should schools be given greater autonomy, or is the experiment in qualified self-government introduced by the Conservatives to be abandoned by the Labour government intent on restoring some power to local government? The questions posed and answers raised by Dick Atkinson deserve a hearing from all sides of the political spectrum here in the UK, and will resonate with readers familiar with other educational systems, as they contemplate the issue of how far local and central government should be involved in education.

As in all Institute publications, the views expressed in this paper are those of the author, not of the Institute (which has no corporate view), its Trustees, Advisers, or Directors.

October 1997   DR JAMES TOOLEY
*Director, Education and Training Unit,
Institute of Economic Affairs
Research Fellow, University of Manchester*

The Author

Dr Dick Atkinson's first book *Orthodox Consensus, Radical Alternatives* was described by Professor Robert Nisbet as helping us to 'see, as no other book makes us see, the utter bankruptcy of conventional sociological theory'. Having taught at Manchester and Birmingham Universities, Dr Atkinson left conventional academic life to found St Paul's Community Education and Development Project in one of Birmingham's inner areas. The Project has won a national reputation through pioneering the raising of educational standards, reducing crime and enabling local people to build their own local associations.

In close liason with St Paul's and other similar projects in different parts of the country, Dr Atkinson now directs The Phoenix Centre, an urban regeneration agency. His most recent publications include: *The Common Sense of Community* (DEMOS), *Radical Urban Solutions* and *Cities of Pride* (Cassell).

Acknowledgements

The ideas contained in this book have germinated over the years from both practical experience and many conversations. Some of the ideas were first explored in my *The Common Sense of Community* and *Radical Urban Solutions*. Here, they are taken further and can be read as a complement to and extension of the White Paper, *Excellence in Schools*.

In addition, the book is a contribution to the conference, Communities of Hope, to be held in Birmingham on 21 February 1998. This conference will consider the enabling welfare state we need to devise in the years after the Millennium. It will look not just at schools, but at the full range of associations and agencies which affect the quality of life for good and ill in this country. Inquiries and bookings can be made by phoning Conference Support International on 0121 776 7799.

I am indebted to a number of people whose thoughts inform the better parts of this book, including Tim Brighouse, Geoff Mulgan, Tom Bentley, Bryan Stoton, John Rennie, Val Hart, Anita Halliday, David Hargrieves, Mohammad Mahboob, Vymal Sharma, Pat Ranahan, Moyra Connelly, Bob Donnally, Neil McIntosh, Chris Woodhead, Charles Handy, David Blunkett, John Patten, Roger Perks, Pat Robinson, Chris Dunkley, Peter Simpson, Liz Jones, Phil Streat, Gill Coffin and James Tooley. They are, of course, not responsible for the way their ideas come together in this book; furthermore, the errors and inconsistencies which remain are mine.

In memory of Mrs Edith Atkinson, a remarkable teacher.

The view I want to put to you is that administration is only safe when it is in the hands of the philosopher and thinker, the teacher and the artist . . . for whom administration exists merely as the instrument for realising quality and value.

Henry Morris

Give a man a fish . . . and you help him a little bit for a very short while; teach him the art of fishing, and he can help himself all his life . . . Supply him with fishing tackle; this will cost you a good deal of money, and the result remains doubtful; but even if fruitful, the man's continuing livelihood will still be dependent upon you for replacements. But teach him to make his own fishing tackle and you have helped him to become not only self-supporting, but also self reliant and independent . . .

Eric Schumacher

Civilisation hangs suspended, from generation to generation, by the gossamer strand of memory. If only one cohort of mothers and fathers fails to convey to its children what it has learned from its parents, then the great chain of learning and wisdom snaps. If the guardians of human knowledge stumble only one time, in their fall collapses the whole edifice of knowledge and understanding.

Jacob Neusner

Executive Summary

The Third Way

Commonly accepted ideas on how to deliver the services of the welfare state are about to change. Throughout the post-war 'consensus' years we have been faced with a simple, two-way choice between the politics of left or right, collectivism or individualism, nationalisation or privatisation, public or private, larger or smaller tax bills, greater or smaller government.

These dichotomies are unhelpful and confusing. There is a radical alternative, a third way which entails using neither the public nor the private sector alone to deliver services. The woefully weakened 'third' or 'community' sector can, if strengthened, play a vital rôle – which also changes the black or white way we view the public and private sectors. The community sector can rejuvenate civil society close at home, where most people, and certainly children, find their identity, well-being and goals.

The advantage is clear. This third sector embodies mutual responsibility which is rooted in local neighbourhoods. It promotes a powerful sense of personal ownership, generates ethical investment, creates civic assets and local pride. It enhances and develops democracy by adding the quality of personal and local communal participation to that of simple representation. It builds the capacity of people to shape and improve the social, economic and cultural quality of their lives, almost imperceptibly moving into a situation in which the state no longer dominates, enabling others in the third and private sectors to provide. This is progress but not privatisation, liberation of untapped skill and energy, not competition. It neither increases nor reduces taxation, but it does change the very nature of government. Indeed, it entails a radical new compact between people and local and central government.

School Autonomy

Every arena in which the state has provided public services for the people must be examined in the light of this radical new third perspective. Frank Field, Minister of State, and the rest of his team at the Department of Social Security, are not the only ones who have to 'think the unthinkable'. So too does Secretary of State for Education David Blunkett and the Department for Education and Employment (DfEE). For, the welfare state was created to get rid of ignorance, as well as poverty, sickness and idleness, in the first half of the century. But the welfare state as then constituted is simply not appropriate to the task of raising standards and creating a lifelong learning process for all.

Just because it was the Conservative governments of the last decade which recognised that standards were too low, bit the bullet and began to reorganise the way education was delivered is no reason for Labour to go back to the way things were when it was last in power in the 1970s. It must go forward, improve upon and complete the task already underway.

There have been three trends in recent years which the new Labour government appears to want to maintain. The first is the recognition that standards in many schools are still too low and do not service either individual, social or national needs. The second is the suggestion that correcting this serious defect entails a much more interventionist rôle for central government, for example through Ofsted – the Office for Standards in Education – and initiatives like the National Literacy Programme. The third is the increasing exercise of direct responsibility by schools. Already government spokesmen have stated that they want 'LEAs [Local Education Authorities] to be required to devolve more power and more of the budget to schools'. Specifically it has been suggested that there should be a 'new national target of 90 per cent of schools' budgets to be delegated' and 'a ceiling of £50 per pupil per year on management and administration costs for LEAs.' Though, as we will see, figures such as these require a good deal of interpretation, they do not square with the belief amongst many LEAs that they are back in a pre-1980s expansionist phase.

This report is unashamedly in favour of school autonomy. Acting *in loco parentis*, schools, not local or central government, are the deliverers of education. They are vital institutions within their communities. They are the only agency through which most people can be encouraged to take responsibility for their children's education. So, everything we do should be directed towards boosting the financial, organisational and technical ability of schools to shoulder this responsibility.

As long as education is publicly funded in the UK there will be a rôle for the state as custodian of the public purse. Supervision of the effective use of public funds in the case of schools entails some sort of system to ensure that those schools are providing the right quality of education. In addition there are a number of issues which are *supra* school. These would probably include bids to central government for funding, resource allocation between schools, admissions and exclusions policies, provision of places, student grants and an overview of Special Educational Needs (SEN).

This is not far removed from the current statutory or mandatory rôle of the LEAs. But the great majority of local authorities go well beyond this rôle via a wide range of discretionary services which are, at best, only partially defined by schools' expressed needs. All too often it is assumed that any initiative must rely on direct delivery by LEA staff. This bears no relationship to the notion of a local authority which enables schools to deliver the education which children deserve and parents and the nation require.

While education is publicly funded, perhaps there needs to be a good national curriculum, Ofsted inspections, various central government initiatives designed to improve the quality of performance, such as Standard Assessment Tests (SATs) and so on. Such central and local government initiatives could enhance and inspire schools. But the way education has been managed by LEAs has hindered the now agreed quest for schools to raise standards. The decades-long relationship between Town and County Hall LEAs and schools has had four damaging effects:

- Nobody knew what an individual school's budget was, still less how it was arrived at. As we shall see, most, including policy makers, still do not.

- The school was dependent on the LEA and unable to deal with management problems. It could pass the buck when things went wrong.

- The LEA held a monopoly over the supply of support services to schools. There were no alternatives to its one-size-fits-all products, which were not necessarily what schools wanted.

- Schools were 'in' but not 'of' the community they served. While the process and physical assets of education ought to be in the control of the consumer, it was run in the interests of the LEA producer.

The Conservative governments of the 1980s and early 1990s tried to rectify these structural and management defects which inhibited schools by breaking the LEA's monopoly. Unfortunately, it offered no new rôle for the LEA and created division and confusion by creating LM (locally managed) versus GM (grant maintained) schools. The new Labour administration should go beyond the LM versus GM debate by making all schools self-governing (SG) and redefining the job description of the LEA. This would have the following beneficial outcomes:

- We would recognise the need to eliminate the considerable differences between what schools get per pupil in different parts of the country. LEAs hold back different amounts. Further, there is a growing dispute about whether they hold back more than the commonly agreed average of 10 per cent or a figure which is more like 30 per cent. For a secondary school costing £2,000,000 for 1,000 pupils at a cost of £2,000 each this represents respectively the holding back of £200 (10 per cent) or £600 (30 per cent) per pupil. Neither sum compares favourably with the £50 which some suggest might be reasonable. But, as we do not know what amount is held back, research which is independent of the LEA is urgently needed to determine what that amount is. Then it will be possible to judge whether it is too much and what should be done with it.

- The Chancellor has said that he cannot find any more money from the taxpayer to spend on education. So, how can what is spent already be allocated more precisely? It is surely right to spend most of it within the classroom or in direct support of it. What is each school's fraction of the money which government makes available for education and how can it be given it? Each school's budget could be worked out on a commonly agreed age- and disadvantage-weighted national formula for each pupil. Once this formula is known then one computer can calculate what each school in the country should have and then that amount can be given to them.

- Schools would then be able to target their own known budget to where it is most needed – the classroom.

- Schools would rely only on themselves to get things right. From being dependent they would become responsible for their achievements or failures and have to exercise their own independent judgement about how to improve.

- Schools would be able to buy services from independent suppliers who would compete with each other to offer a quality product.

- As well as contracting with independent suppliers of services, schools would be able to create their own. A survey recently conducted shows that many schools are beginning to cluster together in groups of, on average, ten: one secondary and nine primaries. If such schools pool just 2 per cent of their budgets they could generate an impressive array of shared services. For example, they could employ a bursar-like figure in the way that independent schools do. This post is vital to hard-pressed heads who are thereby able to concentrate more fully on driving school improvement forward and creating a variety of home-school links which pull family and school together in support of the child. These could include family centres and education enterprise centres which create jobs and training for school leavers.

- Schools would be owned by the community in which they are based – which is what community educationists have always wanted. Rather than being privatised or centralised, education would be localised and placed within the hands of the consumer.

Different schools will respond to independence by using the talents of their staff in different ways. In place of uniform primary and comprehensive secondary schools, which the LEA bureaucrat supplied, will arise schools of distinction and variety. This is a far cry from the simple choice between the academically excellent and the mediocre of yesteryear, which still inhibits clear thinking on the left. It entails different schools helping different children to realise their different aptitudes.

The existing system's dedication to egalitarian uniformity in place of diversity has resulted in the exclusion and marginalisation of the discerning poor and affluent alike. On the one hand, because the state has not recognised or responded to their need, parents in materially poor urban areas have set up their own independent faith and small schools. Unlike their counterparts on the continent, these schools do not have state funds and are run on love as much as money. On the other hand, more affluent parents who chose the old direct grant schools were excluded from the state system and forced to send their children to independent and fee-paying schools.

Yet, the newly diverse state system of schools needs the drive and commitment which both kinds of parent could inject. The reforms we propose not only build variety into the existing one-size-fits-all state system, but enrich it by including within it those schools which were previously excluded and seen as alternatives or rivals to it.

What are the implications of these reforms for the costly LEA empire of the past? As long as it reacted defensively, tried to hold on to its old rôle and compete with new independent suppliers, it was forced to argue that it should consume a disproportionate share of the funds which should have gone into the education of children. Thus it avoided finding a new rôle.

The LEA's tasks of management and the supply of funds to schools have gone. Further, we can see that it would be just as futile for the LEA to try to supply services to schools in competition with private suppliers as it would now be for the government to try to undertake the task of business in the private sector.

So, we must ask: Once shorn of the task of funding schools, managing them and providing them with services, *does the LEA have a function?* One irreducible task which it is argued that local government must perform is to ensure the effective use of public funds, set and monitor standards and inspire schools to achieve them. We also need to know whether all children are receiving an education which their particular needs justify. But, given the national rôle of the DfEE, Ofsted and the curriculum council, these and a number of other residual functions do not justify the retention of a large old-style LEA. There also needs to be a new unambiguous way of funding it that does not force it to take money from schools which should be spent in the classroom.

The specialist departmental empires of local government which the welfare state needed in the first part of the century – when schools had to be built, staffed and managed to cater for the children of growing industrial communities – were one thing. The kind of government now needed in the age of instant information and consumer choice is quite different. The schools are now long built. Their governors and teachers can manage and look after them. Yet, the relatively affluent community around them is unravelling socially, rendering it less able to encourage the child to benefit from school.

It is slowly dawning on us that true welfare cannot be solely supplied by the state, but arises only when ordinary people feel motivated to work with each other at a very local level through 'little platoons' of voluntary and religious associations, self-help groups and schools. Indeed, each school could become a key 'platoon' in its catchment neighbourhood which both educates children and invigorates its community. By returning the assets of education – plant, grounds and staff – to each neighbourhood, people would be offered the hand-up which ownership and pride call forth – just the catalyst which New Labour searches for as it redraws the structure and function of the modern welfare state. We conclude that the Town and County Hall of today needs a quite different kind of enabling and visionary department which ensures that schools set high standards and encourages the development of strong community in support of them.

In response to such questions as these, a few authorities have already merged the functions of their education and social services departments into Children's and Community Services Departments. These could be held up as models which other authorities can follow. They are the harbingers of a new deal between people and the state. They show the way forward for a redesigned post-welfare state.

1 | Introduction

The great reforming governments of Lloyd George and Clement Attlee ensured that we spent the first two thirds of this century building schools for all as part of the welfare state in order to end ignorance as well as poverty, sickness and idleness.

But unintended consequences often bedevil human intention and it is now clear that whatever progress was made by the welfare state must be balanced by the fact that people have become dependent on the state's services and the institutions which it supplies. This has taken from people their sense of responsibility and ability to shape and improve the quality of their lives. In tandem with other dramatic economic and cultural changes, this has resulted in material affluence and social squalor. As with the physical environment, we have come to take more out of the social environment than we put in. We have become poor stewards of the quality of our lives. As Rabbi Neusner warns:

> 'Civilisation hangs suspended, from generation to generation, by the gossamer strand of memory. If only one cohort of mothers and fathers fails to convey to its children what it has learned from its parents, then the great chain of learning and wisdom snaps. If the guardians of human knowledge stumble only one time, in their fall collapses the whole edifice of knowledge and understanding.' (Sachs, 1997, p. 173).

The great challenge which faces us as we end this century is how to reinvent the welfare state (and indeed, go beyond it) so that it releases the energy of individuals and helps people to reach beyond themselves in association with others. We need to build social capital as surely as we used to amass economic capital. This is why the appointment of Frank Field – author of *Stakeholder Welfare* (1996) and *Making Welfare Work* (1995) – to the Department of Social Security is exciting. We know that we have to 'think the unthinkable' in his arena and come up with bold new solutions. But we also need a similar radical thinker in other domestic arenas of state, including local government and education. Can Secretary of State David Blunkett and his colleagues at the Department for Education and Employment also think the unthinkable or will they be prey to Old Labour's collectivist thinking?

Over 20 years ago, Prime Minister Jim Callaghan tried to inject new thinking into Old Labour by calling for a Great Education Debate. But his plea fell on deaf ears and most people in educational circles insisted that 'There is no problem which more money cannot solve.' Few then acknowledged that standards were far too low, that our education system was in need of serious overhaul or that the communities in which schools are embedded were withering on the vine. Attitudes have since changed.

The last 18 years were dominated by Margaret Thatcher and her conviction that our sluggish economy needed to be liberated from an array of collectivist constraints. First, she tackled the attitudes and laws which held back the industry of people in the private sector. She privatised great swathes of the economy. This was resisted by Old Labour, but few people now vote for Arthur Scargill! Baroness Thatcher changed the way we all now think about the economy. Indeed, New Labour was elected in May of 1997 on a manifesto which promised to take Thatcher's economic revolution even further – if that is possible. All are now agreed that market forces are more efficient economically than state planning and that competition and consumer demand are key features in the delivery of choice and the quality products which people expect today.

But many people were eventually touched by the casualties and upheavals caused by economic reforms and, when Prime Minister Thatcher turned her hand to social reform, people who yearned for compassion and co-operation suspected that she merely intended to privatise hospitals and schools, destroy the welfare state and put nothing in its place but raw competition. Her mission foundered and the Conservatives lost power, perhaps for a generation. If, as many people seem to believe, these great swathes of social life are now safe in Labour's hands, because it claims to care for and use them, can ministers achieve the reform which Thatcher began but failed to accomplish – the radical reorganisation of the welfare state?

The Conservative governments of the 1980s and early 1990s made a start. In education, they boldly identified that standards in schools were inadequate and introduced a range of reforms to tackle the problem. They set out a national curriculum which was over-elaborate at first but, most now agree, was much needed.[1] Standard Assessment Tests (SAT's) showed teachers and parents what their children should have learned by the ages of 7, 11 and 14. GCSEs and 'A' levels now give the final public outcome of 11 and 13 years of education in league tables which parents and employees can scrutinise. Her Majesty's Inspectorate was reorganised. In its place Ofsted now inspects every school every 6 years. Failing schools can be closed and inadequate teachers and heads removed.

These are all important steps in the right direction which have, belatedly, convinced most observers that standards are too low and that money alone will not change the situation.[2] These reforms take the unwilling educational horse to water. But, even together, they have not convinced it to drink. Before it will do so it needs to be motivated. It must want to drink. That is, a change in the attitude and culture of schools is required which helps them to see the virtue of those reforms so that they will benefit from them, rather than, as is so often the case, seeing them as unnecessary chores.

If, as we now know, a failing school can be turned round in a few short years by a vigorous head who has a clear policy for school improvement and works with, not against, the above reforms, why is it that all schools do not yet succeed? What is stopping them from achieving this apparently straightforward task?

One answer, which New Labour may be slow to acknowledge because of its affection for LEAs, is that we do not yet have an education system which manages schools in efficient and productive ways. We know that a badly managed and poorly supported team of good football players can lose match after match to a well-led team of inferior players. The same is true of schools. The way we have been managing schools is no longer appropriate. For example, surely the

---

[1] For dissent on this issue, see Tooley (1996), chapter 5.

[2] A revelation supported by Eric Hanushek, a leading American education economist, whose exhaustive survey of academic education literature found no correlation between the amount of public expenditures and student achievements (see Hanushek, 1996).

management of schools should be measured entirely in terms of its beneficial impact on schools? Yet, it is not. There are three key errors in the way schools have been managed by the Education Authorities (LEAs) of our Town and County Halls.

1. LEAs have encouraged the development of spending patterns which are not in any way related to teacher and pupil needs in the classroom. Perhaps the clearest example is in respect of that LEA service which should be most clearly related to professional practice in schools – the advisory / quality assurance services. Some 60+ per cent of school children are in primary schools. Yet, the proportion of staff in advisory services in LEAs with primary expertise is probably less than 10 per cent. As a result of the LEAs' failure to respond to their customers' needs, the great majority of Ofsted primary inspections had to be undertaken initially by people who had never worked at primary level! The author vividly recalls commenting favourably to a head about his LEA advisor's personal abilities. He answered : 'Yes, but he never comes when we want him or does what we want. We have to fit round him and his concerns'. Schools which are managed to a substantial degree by LEAs are in no position to deploy or target their resources to where they are most needed.

2. As a result of not being self-governing, schools have developed a dependence on the LEA which is unproductive. They feel that they cannot cope on their own. This in turn undermines their sense of responsibility for building on their strengths and eliminating weaknesses. They lose incentive and lower their sights as well as missing out on funds and services which they could deploy more effectively than the LEA.

3. The traditional model of organising education ensures that schools are 'in' but not 'of' the community whose children and parents they serve. If we abdicate our responsibility and leave education to specialist bureaucrats and administrators (however enlightened and personable they might be) we will deserve only what they are capable of delivering. In fact, the best start in life for a child is parents who care, and a neighbourhood which cares

passionately about his or her education, personal development and prospects – and has the means to take action to ensure positive outcomes. While there is some truth in the old African saying, 'it takes a whole village to raise a child', it may be more accurate to say that 'parents raise the child, but the village creates the environment and opportunity for the child to succeed'.

The creation of a culture which is supportive to schools can be encouraged at Whitehall and Town Hall level. But, it can only be delivered and brought to life at the level of the actual school, its parents and catchment community. If that school is owned by and part 'of' that community and not just 'in' it, then the child is more likely to be well served and the community will feel that it controls its own educational assets – buildings, grounds and staff – rather than being alienated from them.

So, in addition to the reforms mentioned above, the Conservative governments of the 1980s and early 1990s also tried to tackle the local government monopoly which organised schools and open it up to different ways of motivating and gaining quality support for schools. The Education Reform Act (ERA) of 1988 created two new ways of funding and managing schools. It created grant maintained (GM) schools which gained all the funds available for their pupils through direct funding from central government, thus bypassing the LEA (a notional 100 per cent of their budget). It also created locally managed (LM) schools which are now commonly thought to receive about 90 per cent of their budget through direct funding from the central government, with the old LEA retaining the rest to spend on their behalf. The exciting potential of this government reform was not fully realised, in part, because many people suspected that, like the NHS, the Town Hall and LEA were targets of the government's ideological agenda. Indeed, in analysing the history behind the ERA, researchers have noted the partisan tinge to the effort to defend the LEAs. It is thus less than surprising that LEAs were not given a clear, non-partisan model which showed where the government's reforms were leading, what was expected of them and why.[3]

---

[3] See Fitz *et al.* (1993).

Four key questions arise:

- Now that there is a new Labour government, is it possible or desirable to return to the pre-ERA situation which it last presided over in the 1970s? Or, can it clarify and harness the potential of the reforms which the Conservatives initiated and make them truly beneficial for schools, pupils and their catchment neighbourhoods in today's world?
- Just why did the old Town and County Hall way of managing schools come to fail? What is the best rationale for breaking away from its monopoly of funding, control and provision of services?
- If schools are expected to manage themselves, this will create variety in place of egalitarian uniformity and empower communities. What are the implications of variety and diversity for Labour's thinking? How will stronger communities relate to local government?
- If LEAs and schools both have to change, what are they changing into and what, in future, will be the relationship between them? Indeed, if schools are to become truly self-governing, is there a rôle for the LEA at all? And, if so, what is it? Do rôle models exist which can guide schools and LEAs along the new path?

It is important for all concerned with raising standards in schools to face these questions. The onus is on us to produce practical answers which draw on clear thinking from all quarters, without giving way to one or other of the entrenched sectional interests which so often confuse the educational scene. We have to take a broader and more statesman-like view than any narrow interest will allow. It is my view that, if the culture which drives schools is to change – as envisaged in the Labour Government's first White Paper (DfEE 1997) – then it is also the case that the structures of management which affect that culture must also change.

2 | The Rationale for Moving to Self-Government

Self Reliance and the Modern Business Organisation

To understand the policies and structures which are now needed in the public sector of schools, it is first important to note that the typical private sector organisation's management structure has had to undergo radical change so that it can compete and thrive in the modern post-industrial world.

Charles Handy (Handy, 1989) describes the old industrial business as being shaped like a pyramid, with manual workers at the base of this pyramid, receiving and obeying instructions from a remote head office at the apex of the pyramid. Once, the educated élite who staffed head office might have been thrusting and entrepreneurial in spirit and attitude. Over time, however, they became complacent, immune to change and rule-bound. They failed to inspire and motivate their workforce. Compared with their modern equivalents in the Pacific rim and America, they became uncompetitive and faced closure, unless they were prepared to undergo dramatic change in the form, style and attitude of management.

From being shaped like a pyramid, those organisations which underwent this change have come to resemble a maypole, with a slim and charismatic head office. The new senior managers devolve much of the day-to-day decision-taking process to semi-autonomous and self-governing units which hold the different ribbons of the maypole. Those who hold these ribbons have a similar stake and say in the enterprise as those in the apex. The modern firm which makes this essential but painful change is characterised by key features:

- It has undone the cumbersome rules and regulations of its previously large head office. It has written motivation and innovation into its new *modus operandi*.

- It employs fresh, visionary senior managers and often deploys these out to a carefully redesigned factory floor in order to lead small, semi- or fully autonomous, teams of enthusiastic staff with full responsibility for their own budget.

- It expects these teams to take the initiative and tell head office how to resource them rather than awaiting orders.

- In place of the once dependent, uneducated workforce, it employs fewer, but educated, skilled, self-motivating people who work 'with', not 'for', senior managers. It believes in 'worker control', except that the modern worker works by brain as well as by hand and is, in part, a manager.

- Because the team sees their customer rather than head office as sovereign, great efforts are made to achieve a communally accountable, consistently high-quality product and method of production.

The maypole and its teams of independent 'dancers' are bound together not by the one-way commands and the imposed authority of head office but by a common set of values, ideas which motivate all who associate together with the company. Within each part of the company the aim is to foster self-reliance, autonomy and responsibility. The distinction between the pyramid and maypole like organisation is pictured in Figure 1.

At first only private enterprises were forced by competition to move from model (a) to model (b), from pyramid to maypole. By contrast, public organisations such as local education authorities and their dependent 'families' of schools were slow to follow suit. Protected by their monopolies and insulated from customer and community dissatisfaction, they could afford to remain complacent, offer one-size-fits-all schools and ignore the diverse needs of their dependent customers. Gradually however, governments have been forced to realise that they cannot allow this situation to prevail or the delivery of public services will remain poor, the customer (voter) will complain and the country, like the old business, will become uncompetitive.

Figure 1: Models of Management in Industrial and Post-Industrial Society

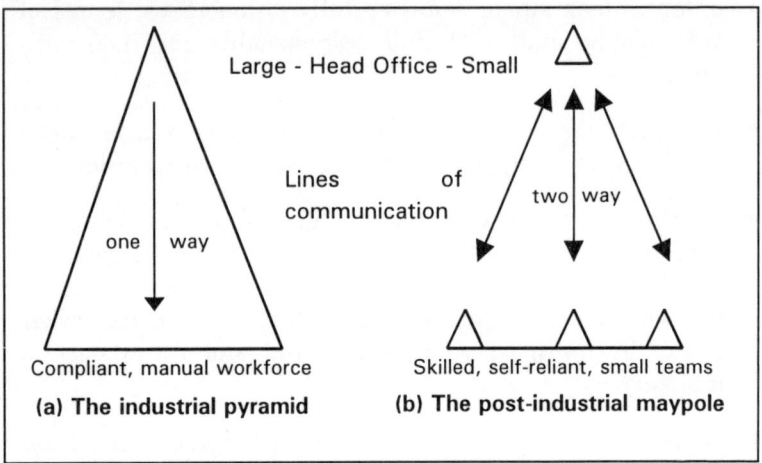

(a) The industrial pyramid (b) The post-industrial maypole

The shift to new forms of government has been taking place across the world for some time. Many countries in Europe already have complex arrangements mixing government provision with the government's purchase of services and their provision by smaller independent voluntary bodies, often associated with the church.

New Zealand and Australia have also seen radical experiments in government. In *Reinventing Government*, David Osborne and Ted Gaebler have synthesised some of these experiences. They show how the pyramid-like, collectivist governments of the industrial age came to both 'steer' and 'row'. That is, they both tried to set aims and goals for people and agencies to follow and also provided and managed the agencies with which they hoped to realise their aims. Because they performed both tasks, governments not only left the productive potential of most people out of their equation, but also failed to perform either task very well.

To be effective, both central and local government are beginning to learn that they must slough off the agencies and services which they have attempted to provide 'for' people and instead enable independent initiative to flourish. Such initiative can take the form of either private enterprise or publicly funded but self-governing agencies, such as hospitals, housing associations and schools. Delegating the 'rowing' function to autonomous, non-governmental agencies, does not necessarily entail 'privatisation'. It merely means giving the initiative and finances for the provision of government-approved services to those self-governing agencies which have the incentive to deliver a good product to the specifications and quality which government lays down.

Government may delegate the task of 'rowing', but it must 'steer' and choose which services are required and to what quality, and it must then, if necessary, raise revenues to pay for them. It cannot delegate the task of 'governance'. This is the special, irreducible task of government. It must set the style and shape of its nation or town. Once freed from the task of 'rowing', a slimmer government can concentrate on the job which only it can do: that of reflecting, co-ordinating and steering the hopes, aspirations and priorities of self-reliant citizens and self-governing private and public agencies.

The Two Cultures and Languages of Dependence and Autonomy

Many state schools have been locked into a pyramid-like relationship of dependence upon their LEA for generations. It is not just the formal power and authority which LEAs have over schools which holds them in its embrace. Most schools also believe in the culture of collectivism and central planning which provides the rationale for the pre-existing way of organising the state system of education. For example, in its criticism of grant-maintained schools, the London Borough of Brent worried that

> 'The ability of an LEA to set up administrative systems according to principles of fairness, reasonableness and the best interests of all schools and all pupils over such crucially important matters as admissions ... and ... central services will become impossible' (Brent Local Education Authority, 1988, cited in Fitz *et al.*, 1993, p. 51).

The culture of dependence tells schools that there is essentially something good about the Town and County Hall's central management of their 'family' of schools. Collectivist arguments sound 'instinctively' better than self-reliant ones because they coincide with the security which the status quo offers and reflect the only experience of 'care and co-operation' which schools have ever known. The Association of County Councils predicted that after passage of The Education

Reform Act (ERA), 'Services which have built up over many years to benefit areas ... would be inevitably disrupted and weakened' (Fitz *et al.*, 1993, p. 52).

Schools may grumble about the poor services which the LEA monopoly used to give them, but they prefer the 'devil they know' to uncertainty and the fear of the unknown. Further, schools could not at first see the virtues of autonomy because they have not been told clearly where it might be leading. Many found it difficult to disentangle the case for autonomy from the perceived Conservative dogma about privatisation and the market place. It seemed to them that they were being asked to move from the monopoly of the pyramid to the anarchy of each for their own, rather than the ordered dance of the 'maypole'.

Perhaps there were reasonable grounds for such fears. For, instead of explaining why it was necessary to move from the old LEA pyramid of controlling and financing schools, to a new, effective and clearly defined 'maypole', the legislation was blurred. The Education Reform Act of 1988 introduced two options. All schools were declared to be locally managed (LM), each with its own governing body and, initially, some 70 per cent of its budget. At the same time, schools were invited to consider becoming grant maintained (GM). If their parents voted to do this then they would gain a notional 100 per cent of their budget, become fully independent of their LEA and relate in future to a quango of Central Government, the Funding Agency for Schools (FAS). Most schools were expected to take this option. It appeared that instead of moving from pyramid to maypole, in which a new, slim, effective head office (the LEA) developed a fresh relationship with its schools, the end point might be no local head office at all combined with centralisation in a branch of Whitehall based in York (the FAS).

At first most schools and educationists resisted both LM and GM. But many schools quickly began to see the practical advantages which LM offered, of semi-independence, some control over part of their budget and, at the same time, the safety of a continuing relationship with their embattled LEA. Only a few heads saw the advantage of full independence, invited their parents to ballot and become GM schools.

With the benefit of hindsight, it is possible to see that the architects of the 1988 legislation did not understand how deeply entrenched the existing 'system' had become. They wrongly supposed that once state schools were formally free to opt out of the state monopoly, then they would immediately clamour to become independent, in the same way that say, a nationalised corner shop might relish the chance of privatisation (see Figure 2, p. 32, below).

In fact, schools which contemplated independence felt exposed and vulnerable. Thus a school which was tempted by GM was easily persuaded that this was analogous to being seduced by the market. The rejected culture and institutions of the LEA merely had to invoke the collectivist culture to shame the school into staying. Such LEAs worked on feelings of guilt and accused the school of greed, individualism, lack of care and so on. The tactics of fear which some LEAs used to bully schools into submission were hardly necessary. Guilt and conscience were more persuasive than brute force.

This approach led to LM and GM being seen as polar opposites. LM was seen by schools as collectivist, 'Leftish' and good, GM as individualistic, Conservative and bad. So the choice of GM inevitably lead to condemnation and conflict. Fitz *et al.* quote one LEA's view that

> 'Once the school had decided to go GM, the Council took the view that the authority would provide only those services it was obliged to provide ... If the school really felt strongly enough to sever its links with the LEA, the Council was not going to restore these links in a different way.' (Fitz *et al.*, 1993, p. 57).

Although it was the culture of dependence and its institutions which imposed this destructive definition onto the situation, it was the would-be independent school which was accused and blamed. One LEA warned that a school that went GM 'has made its bed and must lie in it' (*ibid.*). Therefore, the case for the autonomy of the maypole was wrong footed by a powerful inherited culture and the language of the pyramid. The result was a divided and tense 'system' (see Figure 3, p. 32, below).

Further, when the government insisted that the percentage of the budget given to LM schools should rise to 90 per cent, it became possible for schools to have much of the forbidden fruit without the opprobrium of actually becoming GM. Little wonder that between 1988 and 1997 the movement to GM, which was expected by successive Secretaries of State to accelerate and become unstoppable, slowed first to a trickle then to a halt leaving some 23,000 schools LM and little more than 1,000 GM.[1]

This stalled and conflict ridden outcome was not inevitable or desirable. For, in addition to the example of good business practice and the need to separate the functions of 'steering' and 'rowing', there is also a radical traditional culture and language in this country which reveres the individual, legitimises self-control and independence and which allows people to come together in communities as partners. It welds together the previously opposed virtues of individualism and collectivism.

The Chartists and the Ethical Socialist founders of the Labour Party used this radical tradition to argue their case against the injustice and inefficiency of the uncaring autocratic state of the last century and for the creation of platoons of self-reliant local associations, clubs and unions. Perhaps it is time to resurrect this tradition and show that it provides a better basis for justifying self-government and the local control of schools by communities.

So, it is important for the new government to resist the temptation to move backwards to a pre-1988 situation, take GM schools back into pyramid-like LEA control and halt the developing self-governing logic of LM. Indeed, rather than focusing on the tension and conflict between LM and GM or, as the Labour government's first White Paper (DfEE, 1997) suggests, making the difference between them more acceptable, the time has come to recognise and weld together the virtues in both types of schools.. That is, it is important to move beyond the 'LM versus GM' debate. The issue now is not whether Central government money for schools is best allocated to them through local authorities or a Central government agency (the FAS) but how to:

1) ensure that passing the funds through local authorities does not give them the opportunity to siphon off significant sums before it reaches the schools, thus perpetuating the dependency culture;

---

[1] For a good summary of this decline, see Campbell *et al.* (1996).

2) deliver services to schools more effectively than has been done by the LEAs.

The abandonment of GM status and its replacement by 'Foundation School' status by the new government, as seems to be the intention, could signal a return to the LEA of old. Or, more radically, it could indicate the need to take LM status to its logical conclusion and make all schools neither LM or GM but self-governing (SG).

It is, therefore, most important to stress that the unhelpful models (Figures 3 and 4) are not the only alternatives to the pyramid of collectivism. The effective and radical alternative of the maypole (Figure 5) works to release and combine the virtues of the 'care' of collectivism with the 'autonomy' and self reliance of individualism.

In addition to simply opening the radical option of the 'maypole' by legislation, it is vitally important to offer some detail about how it can work and to provide examples of how, despite the lack of clear guidance from either central or local government, schools are already edging in its direction.

Figure 2: The old collectivist model in which schools are managed by the Town Hall.

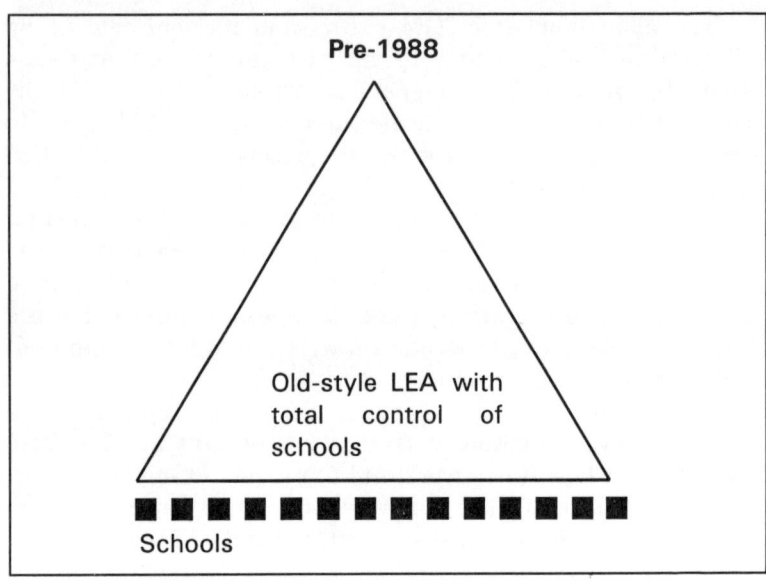

Figure 3: The individualist model in which all schools are GM, the LEA becomes redundant and is replaced by the FAS.

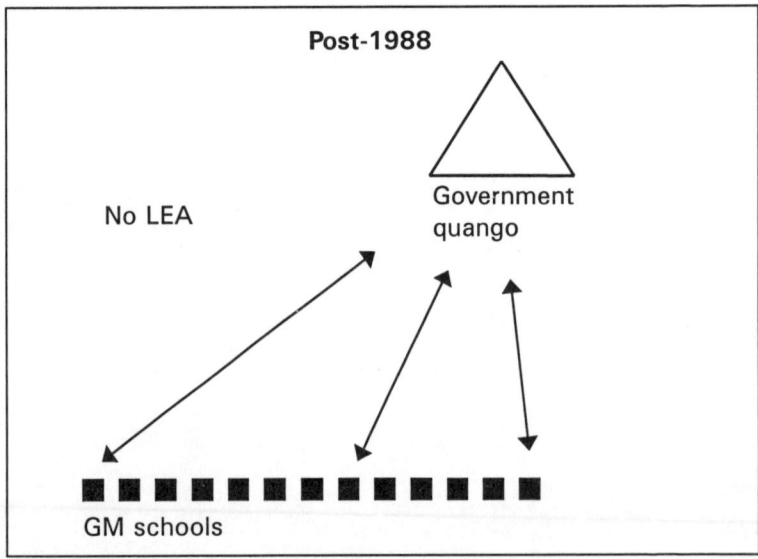

Figure 4: The unintended outcome to date. A two-tier system with conflict and misunderstanding between good LM and GM schools.

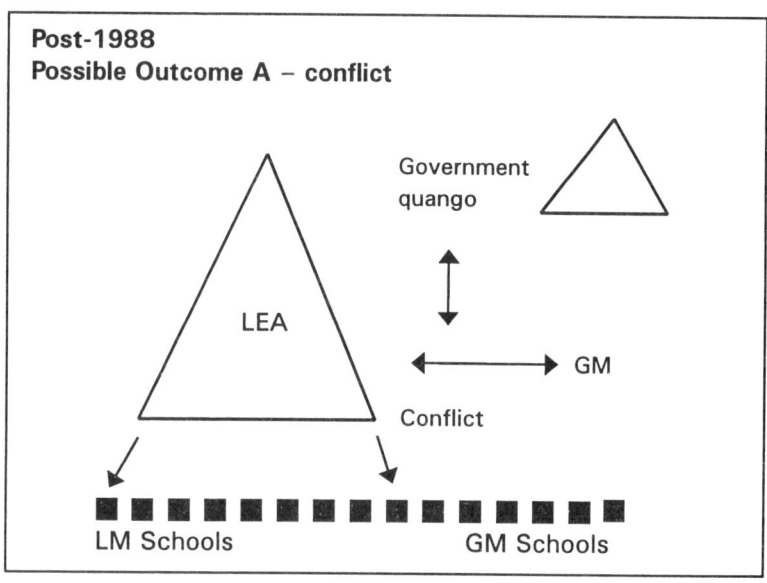

Figure 5: The radical alternative in which the LM and GM are seen as part of a continuum resulting in all schools becoming self-governing, with some services bought from the local authority.

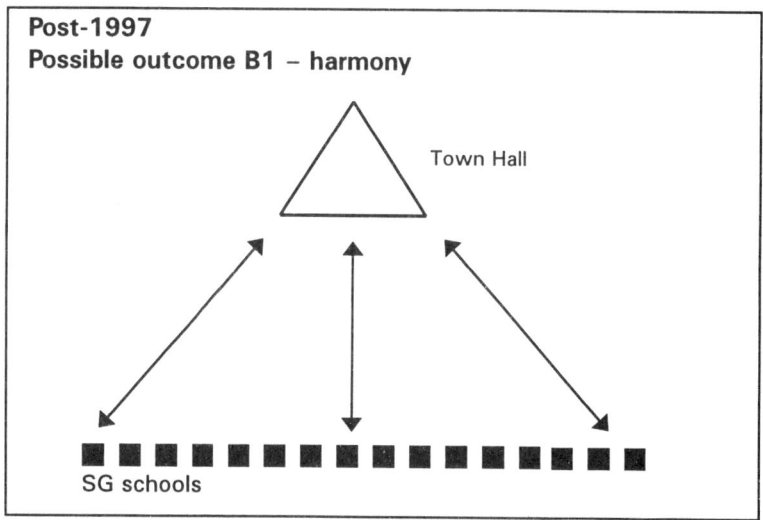

3 | Changing Rôles in Self-Government

We now turn to details of how this new vision can be implemented. First, we look at changing rôles for governors, headteachers and independent suppliers of educational services. Secondly, we point out how much of the education budget seems to get lost within the LEAs, and how recognition of this could transform the education system. Finally, we focus on moves towards the 'clustering' of schools, and show how these developments can be used to reinforce moves towards self-governance of schools.

Governors

Before the 1988 legislation which introduced LM and GM schools, the governing bodies of state schools either did not exist or were ineffective. Those that did exist had no authority and no resources. The LEA monopolised the management of city schools. It was responsible both for the supply of education to the parent customers and for the quality of that education.

The LM/GM reforms gave schools the finance and managerial independence to begin to target resources to the precise needs of their teachers and pupils in the classroom. It gave them freedom from the Town Hall and made them accountable to the parents and neighbourhood in which the school is based.

Governors suddenly became the key to this independence and the new-found accountability of schools to their customers. For they, not the LEA, are now in effect each school's final authority. They, not remote committees of councillors, set the policy guidelines for their school and assist with the major decisions which it has to take. Indeed, in place of a remote Town Hall committee of some 20 councillors, half of whom is in political opposition to the other half, a town with say 100 schools, each with at least 15 governors, now involves 1,500 non-party-political, active citizens in the management of these schools. There is, of course, no reason why the locally elected councillor cannot sit with others on these accountable bodies.

Becoming a governor is an important new form of community service. It enables each school to become owned and controlled by the community. It strengthens the community and returns to it assets, buildings, employees and an educational process which for decades had been the disenfranchising province of remote civil servants.

However, the status of governors is not yet secure. Too many professionals in education view them as 'part of the problem'. In part, this is because not all governors receive enough support and training to give them the confidence to encourage the good headteacher, dismiss or call for improvement from the poor one, reflect the interests of the local customer – the child, parent and community – and stand back when appropriate. However, the belief that there is not enough expertise and energy in neighbourhoods to do the job is a counsel of despair. The voluntary sector of local associations and community groups is highly developed and has a well-honed model of sound self-governance. It has a great deal to teach education and educationists who have not yet recognised the potential created through seeing schools as being a key part of the community sector.

Headteachers

Previously headteachers were dependent, their identity, performance and accountability submerged within the LEA monopoly. They had little room to show initiative. If mistakes were made and standards were low, then the LEA not the school could be blamed. The poor headteacher was hidden, invisible. Now, headteachers are exposed. They no longer have the LEA to blame if things go wrong. Once dependent, with the support of their governors they now need to act as independent educational entrepreneurs.

When GM came, the boldest took that opportunity to create and develop the good school. The best of the rest are making the most of LM. But large numbers now flounder and are at a loss to know how to seize the advantages before them. So, it is important to ask :

- What makes a good enterprising headteacher?

- In future how can they be recruited and trained – in large enough numbers to replace those who cannot make it?

- What can be done with the failing headteachers – either to support them or remove them?

These three questions all need to be answered and solutions put in place swiftly. But they all beg a further question:

In the post-LM/GM era of SG schools and a different kind of LEA, how can the well-recruited, trained and enterprising head be best supported? Are they and their schools now to be seen as totally independent agencies which must fend for themselves in the new rigours of the education market place? Are they to get support and services from a market-style LEA? If so, of what kind? Or, will they find comfort in a mutually beneficial relationship with their nearest school neighbours?

Perhaps the most serious defect of the LM/GM reforms was the lack of any guidance of the kind which could have helped the relationship between schools and LEAs to develop with confidence and clarity. Simply, they were left to fend for themselves. So, most headteachers quite literally kept their heads down, waited to see what might happen while trying to meet the paperwork and targets set by the National Curriculum. Most LEAs fought an anxious, defensive, rearguard action as their once huge empire crumbled with little prospect of an exciting new commonwealth emerging to make sense of and offer hope for the future. One outcome was that headteachers did not immediately see that they could use their delegated budget to trade with a new breed of independent supplier of services rather than rely on those which LEAs hoped to continue to supply.

Independent Suppliers of Educational Services

Before the Education Reform Act the LEA controlled all the support services which heads and schools needed. For example, it provided curriculum support and teachers of specialist subjects, advisors, replacements for teachers who were sick or on study or parenting leave. It provided buildings and their maintenance, grounds and their maintenance, caretakers, cleaners and caterers – in a word, it provided everything. The pyramid of local government really did 'row' as well as 'steer'.

The real costs of these services were high but hidden within the LEA's overall budget. And, because there was no competition for these services, they were often of a poor or indifferent one-size-fits-all quality, the educational equivalent of national health spectacles and uniform housing estates. Certainly they did not fit the particular needs of individual schools. But before the ERA reforms, the schools had to accept what they were given. However, once schools gained control over part of their budget two alternative sources of supply were opened up.

- Schools could create their own support services or provide something qualitatively different for the same price.

- Schools could buy in their own support services from a new breed of independent suppliers which competed with the LEA's services in terms of price and quality.

We will consider the supply of independent services and their implications for the best method of funding schools before exploring how schools themselves can play a vital part in providing their own quality service.

A good example of the kind of poor service offered was when schools sought temporary teachers from the LEA. The headteacher who learned in the evening, weekend or holiday that a teacher would be absent on Monday had, during the decades of LEA monopoly, to wait until after 9.00 a.m. on Monday morning before the LEA's phone might be answered. As many headteachers were then ringing the same number it could take hours just to get through. Finally, on Wednesday a teacher of, say, physics would arrive to teach English just at the moment that the previously indisposed teacher returned. The service did not deliver and was, therefore, a drain on scarce resources, time and energy – for both LEA and school.

Now, however, independent suppliers of replacement teachers answer the phone at any time of the day or night and guarantee that suitably qualified specialist staff will be present as and when schools require.

Take also the case of grounds maintenance. Before, many schools reported that they could not tell that any work had been done on their grounds. Now schools can buy in independent contractors and hold them to the specifications of their contracts. When an independent grounds maintenance contractor put in a bid of £15,000 to one school whose LEA had previously charged £19,000, suddenly the cost of the contract was reduced to £5,000 and the Local Authority was again awarded the contract. Yet, for £5,000, the grounds were maintained rather better than had been the case when the job was supposed to cost £19,000.

Because schools can now buy in services ranging from supply teachers and grounds maintenance to financial and specialist teacher support, new providers have arisen to supply the demand. So, in place of services given to schools by a monopolistic LEA supplier, whether they wanted them or not, schools can now choose the best from a variety of competing, independent suppliers. As they lose function after function to independent suppliers of quality services, LEAs are left wondering what rôle they might play in the post-LM/GM era. Unfortunately, few have yet made the imaginative leap to define a bright new 'steering' rôle for themselves. Too many still try to cling defensively to their pyramid-like rôle of 'rowing' as well as 'steering'.

LEAs and Diminishing Education Budgets

Currently, the typical LEA says it retains 10 per cent of each school's budget to help it to administer it and delegates 90 per cent to the school. The typical secondary school of around 1,000 pupils receives a delegated budget of £2,000,000 and a primary school of 400 pupils receives around £700,000. Thus, the LEA retains respectively £222,222 and £77,777: not insignificant sums. This equates to roughly £200 per pupil, rather more than the £50 per pupil which some politicians now believe it should be.

Several key players are interested to know exactly what amount of money the LEA should retain, if any. Schools are just one of these. If they had more money, some would go on books and teachers, some on buying more services. The independent suppliers of services are another. They could offer more if they could win more contracts. The new government is equally concerned; the Chancellor of the Exchequer has said: 'No more money for education. If you wish to improve standards do not throw more money at it. You will not get any. Use existing money in more effective ways.'

Of course, the LEAs are also an interested party. The more funds they can retain from schools, the more they can sustain their existing sphere of influence, jobs and status. So, it would not be surprising if LEAs managed to both hang on to what is said to be their current share of the finances (10 per cent) but so arranged the figures that they retained more than that. In an astonishing paper, *School Funding*, Nick Seaton has suggested that the established story may be so distorted by LEA accounting as to be fictitious (Seaton, 1996).

He argues that LEAs do not retain just 10 per cent of the funds potentially available to schools but, on average, 30 per cent. That is, if all the funds potentially available to schools, but which is retained, were added up for the typical secondary and primary school it would not equal the figures given earlier, but £857,000 and £300,000.

This sum, Nick Seaton calculates, is the equivalent not of the £200 per pupil mentioned above, but, on average, an extra £594 per pupil – a considerable addition to the amount which schools currently receive per pupil. If Seaton's figures are correct, those who argue that teachers and schools are hard pressed because they have no resources, facilities or books and require extra funding to perform well, are mistaken. All that is required to resource schools well is, as the Chancellor urges, to use existing funds differently, to redirect them from the bureaucracy of the LEA to schools which can then target them to their own distinctive needs.

Seaton's report was published by the Centre for Policy Studies (CPS) which is associated with the Conservative Party, and no doubt some will be suspicious of the figures on this account. It is important that these figures are double-checked; initial work has been undertaken by a firm of management consultants commissioned by the Centre for British Teachers (CfBT), an educational charity. Their findings as well as Seaton's calculations are outlined in the Appendix. Here it is sufficient to record that:

- The consultants conclude that the figures are 'spot on' and that by deducting 20 per cent of the money available to them for education before they take the commonly known sum of 10 per cent, LEAs are preventing a proper 'mixed economy of service provision from developing'.

- The sums need to be further researched before they will be believed across the political spectrum. Steps are already being taken to check them in four test-case authorities with the help of a nationally recognised firm of accountants.

- The case for a nationally agreed value-added, pupil-led funding formula for schools is becoming irresistible. Provided that this formula includes an agreed age weighting and acknowledges an increase for the degree of deprivation of its pupils, each school's full budget could be calculated by one computer based anywhere in the country. Each school, its headteachers and governors would then know precisely what their annual budget should be. A cheque could then be allocated to each school on a quarterly basis either via the LEA or the computer which does the calculation.

Is Seaton's work correct? Are schools really missing out on 30 per cent of their budget, £594 per pupil? If so, what proportion of this money would have to be spent on essential non-classroom-based activities and what proportion could be diverted right into the classroom? Answers to these questions must now be provided as a matter of urgency. If these answers are to be clear and unambiguous they must be provided by neither the CPS nor LEAs but by independent accountants whose judgements can be trusted by everyone.[1]

Such accountants should also examine the little known 'SSR' – the Service Strategy and Regulation. This is another item of local authority 'creative accounting'. Even if all schools opted out, the LEAs realised that there would still be much left for them to do: there would be legal questions to answer, buildings to inspect, CEOs to employ, and all manner of other things. Hence it was decided to create an SSR budget that does not even appear in a LEA's budget. This means that rather more than 30 per cent of the potential budget for each school is withheld by local authorities. But in the case of the

---

[1] The relevant research has not yet been completed, so this Paper makes the conservative assumption in calculations which follow that LEAs are only retaining 10 per cent of the funds potentially available to schools. If this figure later turns out to be 30 per cent it will then be a pleasant bonus.

SSR it is entirely invisible to schools and educationalists. Few, if any, even know of its existence. The total sum that is withheld from schools nation-wide could equal as much as £2 billion.[2]

Towards a National Funding Formula

Some have argued that a national funding formula would be politically impossible to deliver – however fair such a formula may appear. They say that the present, arbitrary LEA-led way of funding schools results in great disparity between schools in different authorities. The application of one national standard would mean that, while some schools gain, others will lose, hence the political difficulty of introducing it.

Yet, the introduction of LM in the 1980s was successful despite the fact that each LEA had to cope with exactly this problem within their catchment area. Even more significantly, if schools were given the whole of their fair share of the available funds without being 'top-sliced' by their LEA, very few, if any, would loose funds altogether. It would, in my opinion, be very popular.

None the less, rather than introduce the national formula for all schools at once, it might first be piloted (as LM was first piloted) in a limited number of areas so that it could be seen to be to the advantage of all. We will return to this possibility below.

The First Steps towards Clustering – Schools Providing Services for Themselves

Interestingly, at the same time that new suppliers of services were arising and schools were beginning to exercise their new found independence by trying to buy from them, some schools also realised that they could act together without reference to the LEA.

They began to look tentatively sideways at their neighbours. How were they coping? Could they learn from each other's good and bad practice? As there was so little left after staff salaries were raised, could some items or services be shared? In 1985 the Fish Committee suggested that secondary schools and their feeder primaries should form into clusters and collaborate in meeting their pupils special

---

[2] I owe this insight to Graham Jones and Andrew Turner.

educational needs by sharing resources. This co-operation, Lunt *et al.*, report in their book *Working Together* (1994) 'would be cost effective ... [and] the gap could begin to be closed between LEA determined support and support provided on the initiative of schools'.

Some commentators have suggested that schools' interest in clustering illustrates the need for an LEA. No one denies that certain services are best delivered beyond the level of the individual school. The crucial point, however, is that in this model the schools are in charge and can either buy services from independent suppliers and from LEAs or provide them themselves. In a word, they create their own supply. But, because it is their own scarce money they are using, there is no potential for the interests of educational bureaucracies to prevail over those of schools.

A 1996 survey carried out on behalf of the author by the CfBT asked all of the schools it had inspected whether they had come to share any facilities with their neighbours. Nearly half (145) replied. Of these, 63 (43 per cent) said that they now shared some facilities, while of those that did not 50 (34 per cent) said that they would like to. Only 25 (17 per cent) said that they did not and would not like to. The impulse to share – at 77 per cent – was substantial. As the bar chart below indicates (Figure 6), a wide range of facilities was shared by the 63 schools. Each school typically shared three facilities and could envisage sharing more. While 50 per cent shared training and sporting activities, relatively few (eight per cent) shared time where one Head represented others at meetings and passed on to colleagues the information gained.

Clusters varied from containing just two schools to 17, with the average being 10. Not everyone within a cluster shared everything. So, say, five of the 10 might share maintenance while all might share in training. Schools termed their association with neighbouring schools differently – families, patch-based groupings and pyramids, as well as clusters. A typical 'pyramid' – clearly reminiscent of the 'maypole' model outlined earlier – entailed one secondary relating to its feeder primaries as shown by Figure 7.

Only 26 per cent of those schools which clustered had designated a member of staff other than the head to be responsible for overseeing shared facilities and none reported that they had created a special post to develop cluster facilities. It seems that those who carry this interesting new burden do so on top of an existing time-table.

Figure 6: Percentage of schools sharing different facilities

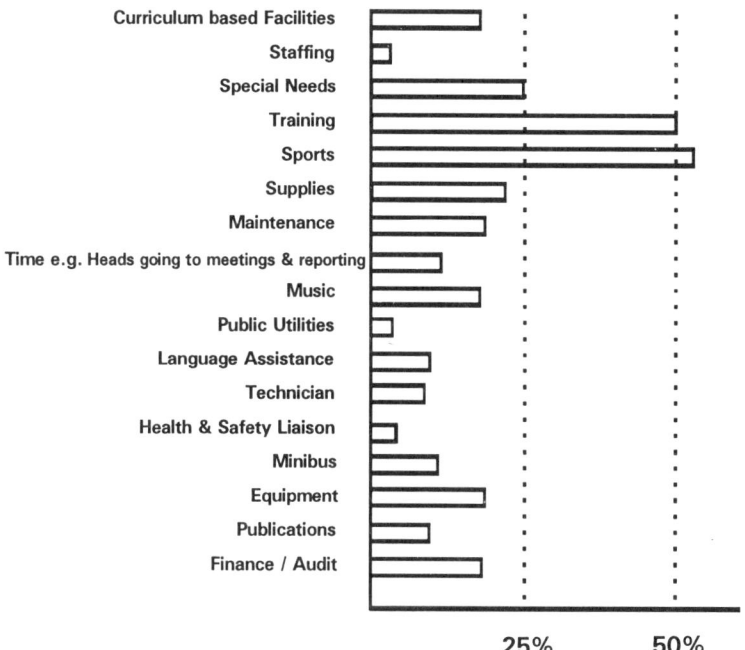

Figure 7: A typical cluster pyramid

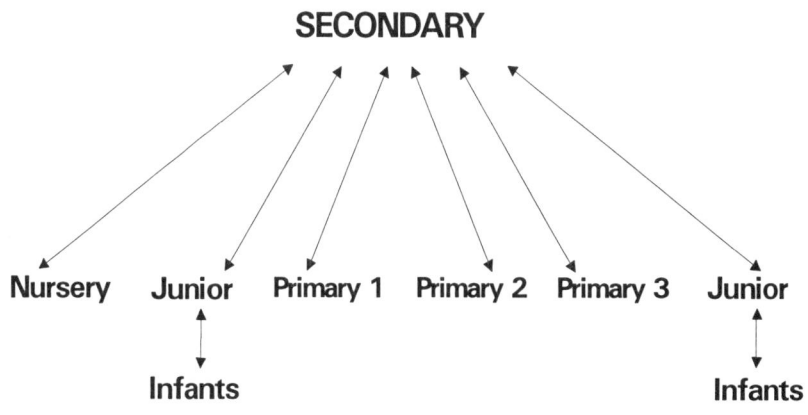

Aware that most schools do not at present think that their budget could possibly allow a school to appoint a specialist cluster facilitator, CfBT's Trust also granted two separate clusters in Birmingham the funds to create their own special post for a three-year period which started in 1995/96. While one of these clusters still sees its facilitator as a 'project' which may or may not continue when the three-year grant ends, the other has already built its new post into the budgets of its schools and its *modus operandi*.

In future, these schools say that they will fund the cost of the post themselves because of the mutual benefits which have arisen, which they now regard as indispensable to their development. This cluster has even negotiated the closure of a small nursery school with its LEA and has reopened these premises as a shared cluster facility in which joint projects, teacher and governor training and other events take place. The facilitator of this cluster (the head of its secondary school who took early retirement) is now seen as 'indispensable'. Without him, the clusters could not sustain or develop their shared activities. Indeed, both CfBT-supported clusters have formed a cluster development plan which is reviewed and updated from time to time in just the way schools now individually operate with a development plan. The cluster plans cover sharing in training, language development, home-school liaison, discipline, attendance, curriculum development, joint project work, equipment and information (see Figure 8).

This means that we can develop the structural model of our educational system so that it looks like neither a pyramid nor centre-less 'anarchy', but like the maypole: (see Figure 9).

It is understandable that few other clusters of schools have developed the range of shared, targeted facilities as have these two pilots. But our survey reveals that more and more appear to be tentatively moving in that direction. How much faster might they move if they had an enterprising head, a supportive governing body, their full budget to play with, a cluster facilitator to guide them, a few more good and well-documented working models to emulate and an encouraging LEA and government? How might this possibility be realised?

Figure 8: The cluster model.

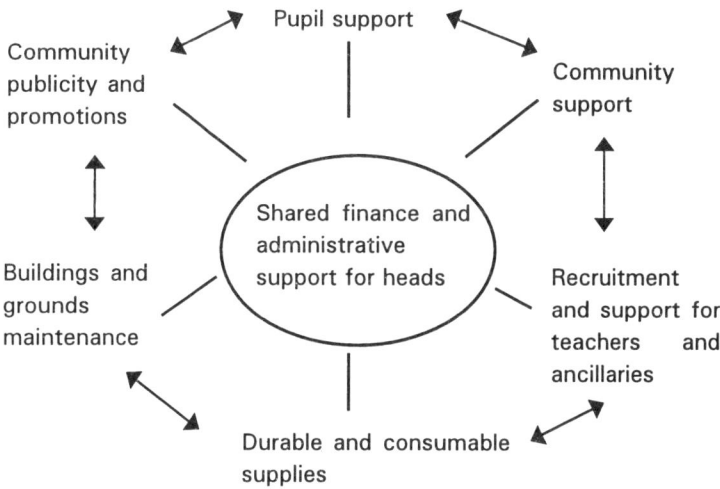

Figure 9: The maypole system.

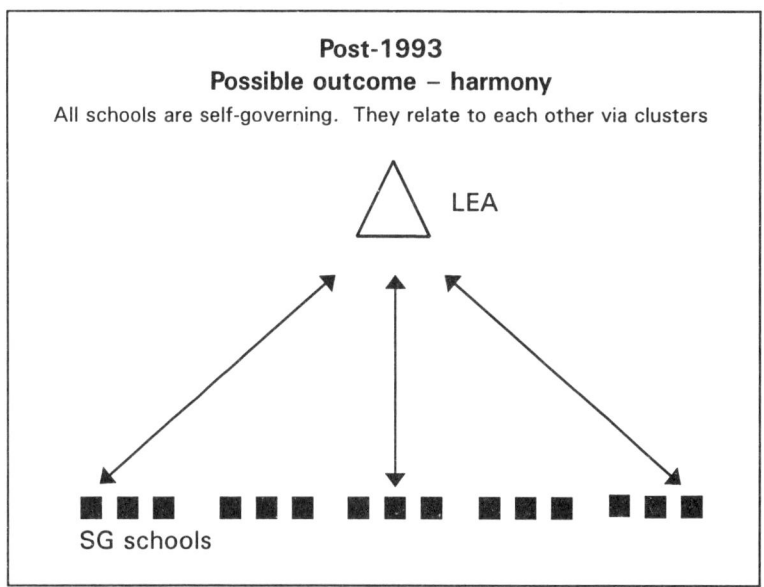

Administration and Cluster Development

In the past the LEA performed the administration and management tasks for all schools. So a primary school only needed to have a part- or, at the most, a full-time secretary. A large secondary school might have had two or three secretaries. Post-LM/GM, however, the governors, head and senior staff have acquired the new rôles of management and development to add to the vital tasks of teaching and leadership. Thus, life in the modern school office and Head teacher's room has become hectic. So, important opportunities have been missed, or indefinitely deferred.

The rôle of the head and senior colleagues has enlarged from that of leader and organiser of teachers to include the old LEA tasks of finance officer, computer operator, manager, administrator, servant of the governing body, marketing and promotions officer and, it seems, cluster facilitator. Yet, no additional staff have been allocated to help the headteacher to remain on top of this increased range of duties. Instead of rising to this challenge and the opportunity it presents to improve the quality of the school's performance, this has led many to complain: 'Teaching used to be fun. Now it's changed. I'm never in the classroom. The job is now full of chores and holds no pleasure.'

Of course, independent schools and free-standing colleges which have never depended on or been serviced by LEAs have long had non-teaching administrators and departments of administration which leave the teachers and lecturers free to get on with the task of teaching and research. Perhaps it is time that state-funded self-governing schools were allowed to follow suit.

Some suggest that the enterprising headteacher will be helped if the first new post which a new self-governing school creates is that of finance officer or bursar.

This is not necessarily so. The headteacher and senior staff may find that a good administrator, manager or development officer is of much greater value as well as a real relief to them personally. On reflection, schools may feel that a bursar is not necessary and that a finance officer will suffice.

The new postholder(s) can relieve heads and senior staff from some of the burdens of time-tabling, and a host of important paperwork chores. They might negotiate the contract for school meals, caretaking and cleaning. Indeed, they might not only administer these resources but assist with their supervision. Their brief would be to help the head to target every available resource to the needs of the classroom and the school as a whole in conjunction with its neighbours.

In *The Mosaic of Learning*, David Hargreaves compares schools with hospitals (Hargreaves, 1994). Less than half the staff of hospitals are consultants and doctors. Their expertise is carefully targeted to the health needs of patients. They are supported in this task by an array of other, less costly, but no less important, assistants – sisters, nurses, orderlies, paramedics, social workers, administrators, porters, cleaners and so on.

In inefficient contradistinction, the school is made up almost entirely of costly teachers who in addition to teaching – the task for which they are expensively trained – also act as the educational equivalent of sisters, nurses, orderlies etc. This is not only financially but educationally inefficient. The new administrator, cluster facilitator rôle and cluster development plan we describe could and should herald the possibility of reorganising the way schools appoint and deploy their staff.

The specialist task of helping heads with administration, development, quality assurance, marketing and so on, is a new one in state schools. It is quite different from the rôle associated with the LEA administrator or inspector. So it needs piloting on a wider stage than that provided by the CfBT experiment. Further, specialist support and training facilities need to be made available both to the new postholder and to headteachers and senior managers, in order to help them to manage the post properly.

It is now clear that the devolution of finance and control to self-governing schools gives them the responsibility and the means to manage their own affairs. But, this responsibility can only be exercised effectively if the administrative and managerial rôle, and the funds which pay for it, are relocated in schools and cluster of schools. Each school and cluster needs its own officer and new colleagues to assist heads and senior management to exploit the advantages of devolution to the full, without creating overload.

However, because they have not had such a development post or the vision and extra dimension of thinking which it brings to a school, many hard-pressed headteachers continue to have their eyes diverted by all the other tasks which jostle for their attention and drag them reluctantly from the classroom. Yet, the devolved budgets of the self-governing school provide it or group of schools with an important opportunity. They do not need to wait for government or their LEA to grant them the post. They can create it themselves. But how, when so many think that there is so little room for manoeuvre in their individual school's budget?

Co-operation and Clusters

It is important to recall that each secondary school is delegated from the LEA on average approximately £2,000,000 and each primary £700,000. After teacher salaries are accounted for and other essential services are paid for this leaves little slack. But suppose our cluster of 10 schools pools just 2 per cent of each school's budget. This would then amount to £166,000.[3]

Very many valuable, shared staff or activities could be bought in or created by a cluster of schools with such a sum of money. In addition to the otherwise difficult to fund administrative or development officer, it would be possible to conjure with special needs, specialist subject areas, pre-school, home school, work experience, quality advice, grounds and building maintenance and development, as well as a range of material resources, such as printing facilities – indeed, the full range of facilities indicated by our survey as being of interest to schools.

Staff from a group of schools in Oxfordshire meet regularly to discuss the management of learning and behaviour. Teacher exchanges between the secondary and primary schools are regular. Curricular strengths and weaknesses are targeted. Joint working groups exist in physical education, Craft and Design Technology and English. New departures will presently include working groups in all areas of the curriculum, partnership purchasing and joint school meals and grounds maintenance contracts.

The possibilities here are tremendous. For example, in addition to these facilities, an advanced cluster might see itself as a teacher training centre and develop excellence in

---

[3] £40,000 + £14,000 x 9 = £166,000.

specialist areas of teaching, which might attract the interests of schools from other areas.

Schools can do far more by linking together in fresh ways, than by going it alone. Two examples can be given of what could be gained by 10 schools sharing just 2 per cent of their budgets:

EXAMPLE 1

A Cluster development officer	£30,000
A language development specialist	£20,000
A science specialist	£20,000
Shared administration	£13,500
A network of in-service courses	£20,000
An Inspector/Advisor, or 6 pre-school school workers, or part time specialists, from music to special needs	£40,000
Shared resources; van, printing, publicity, painting and decorating	£22,500
Total	**£166,000**

EXAMPLE 2

A Cluster development officer	£30,000
Shared administration	£13,500
Resourcing meetings of the staff of the ten schools	£2,000
Teacher exchanges and materials	£1,000
Working groups	£1,000
Part-time specialists – 11 @ £6,600 each	£66,000
Community education specialist	£22,000
Parent-involving activities	£20,000
Termly home-school newspaper	£5,000
Cluster marketing brochure and recruiting conference	£5,500
Total	**£166,000**

Rather than trying to do every thing at once, a school or set of schools might wish to start with a competent cluster development officer to help them build slowly and by degrees towards more ambitious targets. Indeed, even before a cluster is formed, a secondary school might lend its feeder primaries its new finance/administration officer.

This new type of post enables a set of schools to:

- Save the finance for the post within a year by careful planning.

- Undertake joint purchasing from independent suppliers as part of this planning process.

- Gradually increase and manage the range and quality of shared support staff and resources for teachers.

- Gain a greater sense of common purpose, mutual support and high morale.

- Take the strain from headteachers and senior managers.

- Use existing money in innovative ways which enables schools to make the very best of what is available to them.

A Possible Future – Schools and Clusters as Family Centres for their Neighbourhood

While different clusters may choose to develop excellence in different curricular areas – arts, technology, science, sports, etc. – they may also choose to achieve a reputation in helping parents to gain the confidence required to give their children the incentive at home to work hard at school. For, the more that the home pulls in the same direction as the school, the more the child and school benefits.

In modern times, communities have become weak and the 'gossamer strand' of experience – and extra pairs of hands – which the extended family once gave parents have been lost. The pre-school teacher could be a vital link between the floundering mother and father and others in the community who can help. The school and its cluster of schools could build on existing networks of child-minders, playgroups and nurseries. Toy, book and resource libraries could help show parents how to talk to and care for their children. Other parents can offer support as well as ideas and suggestions for everything from healthy diet to the best means of controlling difficult behaviour.

The school, like the doctor's surgery or health centre, is a natural meeting place for parents of young children – they go there frequently. Indeed, in some places, the surgery and health centre could also be integrated within the school to form a 'Family Centre'. The more prepared the young child becomes in its pre-school years, the more the school can make rapid progress when the child starts its formal school life. In return, the more the child is able to progress at school, the more the parent is able to cope and help the child to make progress at home.

It is thus possible to envisage the nursery and primary school as being not just the 'provider' of education to young children but also a centre for the whole family. Indeed, the nursery and primary school could combine the functions of education with those of social and health care, advice and training in parenting and employment skills. This could help children to learn early about the realities and responsibilities of adult life.

To facilitate and accommodate the Family Centre, each nursery and primary school would needs a modest suite of rooms in which the rôles of the priest, teacher, social worker, doctor and policeman can intertwine. Indeed, the Family Centre could become the focal point for a kind of informal college of life-long learning and mutual support for the entire area.

Imagine for a moment that the cluster of schools is interlinked via telecommunications networks to a range of educational programmes and specialist teaching centres, able to complement the teacher in the classroom. Then, suppose that the schools are linked via cable to every home in the neighbourhood and to the local college which has devolved and outposted its adult training programme into each of the Schools-as-Family-Centres. What Prime Minister Harold Wilson achieved with the help of television in the 1960s in launching the Open University could be multiplied by the power of the computer and the cable. Today, it is entirely possible to use a cluster of schools both on a conventional 9.00 a.m. to 3.30 p.m. basis and, more efficiently, to deploy their resources around the clock in a cradle-to-grave, open-access college in which the entire neighbourhood is welcomed.

Secondary-aged children as well as adults might gravitate to the exciting, close to home Family Centre and neighbourhood college if they can use it as a home/school study centre. Too many youngsters do not have the space at home to do serious homework and may need expert help from time to time which parents cannot give. While their secondary school might be too far to go for a couple of hours study in the evening, the local Family Centre could present the right atmosphere. If clusters could help one or more of their schools to become a Family Centre or a Home/School Study Centre at the hub of a life-long learning process, they would become the popular focus of a vigorous community. The educational progress which would follow in the wake of friendly competition between various clusters all striving for excellence in these fields, would be substantial.

Educational Enterprises

Some schools, especially secondary schools, have become very enterprising. Like Garibaldi school near Nottingham under the leadership of Bob Salisbury, they raise funds by letting their premises as a conference centre, do outside catering as an extension of food technology, help to train trainee teachers and so on. This is only the start of what is possible.

There is an interesting alternative to using a small but significant part of each school's budget to buy in independent suppliers to provide them with such services as grounds maintenance, buildings maintenance, painting and decorating, printing, catering and so on. They could start their own Education Enterprises Company (EEC) and use it to supply these services themselves. Housed in local premises, like the old nursery school which one of Birmingham's clusters uses, a cluster's EEC could fulfil several purposes. It could:

- Provide good, home-grown, services.

- Keep the costs of those services within the cluster by funding the EEC.

- Create local jobs.

- Use those jobs as 'education-by-doing' devices to guide work experience placements from years 10 and 11 and from school leavers in welfare to work projects.

The local college is likely, for example, to run courses in bricklaying, painting and decorating and so on, but to have few real outlets for their trainees to practice on with lasting effect. The cluster of local schools and other local voluntary associations are obvious locations on which trainees and apprentices can work, so gaining the pride which comes from gainful employment.

A cluster of schools which runs a successful 'EEC PLC' need not stop at sharing services which its members need. It could supply services to other players in its catchment area, such as housing associations and businesses. A state school or cluster of schools which operates in this enterprising way could by those means soon match the investment and endowment funds with which private schools give bursaries or build a new science block or swimming pool. Once released from the dependent, one-dimensional mode of thought of the pyramid, in which schools receive orders and do not set fresh visions for what is possible, the sky becomes the limit.

Self-Government and Community Education and Development

Some say that 'community education' is primarily concerned with opening school buildings in the evenings and weekends for scout groups, wedding receptions, adult education courses, and the like. Others say that a school cannot be a community school unless it has a pre-school worker or a home/school liaison teacher who involves parents in the life of the school and helps the school to reach out to parents and the wider community. Both these definitions are useful, but they do not get to the heart of the matter. For they view community education as being an additional or bolt-on extra, to the 'real' 9.00 a.m. to 3.30 p.m. task of education and school life. Community education is seen as a valuable addition to the educational process in the classroom, but it is not a vital part of that process.

However, community education can be at the very core of the process itself – *the* way of defining good education. It is unlikely that any school can function well, excite teachers and pupils, unless the whole school becomes an extension of the life of the community and that community gains a sense of ownership over and pride in its school.

The best education entails a full-blooded partnership between home, school and the community in which each plays a positive rôle which acknowledges and involves the others.

Indeed, the National Curriculum itself can be brought to life, seen as an integrated whole, through the school's careful study of all aspects of life in the community. In turn, good schools can reflect, support and enhance the values and *raison d'être* of the social life in which they are situated.

Community education need not simply be another task with which the already hard-pressed teacher must grapple. Rather, it can be a vision of education which makes coherent sense out of the reforms that the governments of the 1980s and 1990s made. It can turn a host of chores into an excitement of common purpose and excellent results.

For decades, community educators have tried to capture what Henry Morris meant when he said that the best school lies 'athwart' its community and provides it, like the church or mosque, with a mirror which reflects its identity and a dynamo for driving its development forward. There have been many valiant attempts to achieve this aim and some exceptional successes. However, most of these have foundered on the fact that hitherto state schools have not belonged to their community. They have been 'in' it but not 'of' it. They have been built and controlled by the distant local authority. There has always been a space, even a credibility gap, between them and their pupils and the community.

The 1988 Education Act which created LM and GM schools, implicitly returned the assets of teachers and school buildings to their neighbourhoods. They became accountable to parents and the community through their elected governors. This transformed the situation. Now a self-governing school really can be part of the community. It is owned and controlled by it. Although the government of the day did not necessarily intend to create a situation in which every school could, quite literally, become a community school, it nonetheless did so. The government of today can and should make the point explicit, encouraging and identifying models of good practice which others can emulate.

4 | Choice and Diversity and the Virtues of Self-Government

Variety Is the Spice of Life

Having shown how moves towards self-government could lead to the clustering of schools and facilitate genuine community education, we move on to complete the picture of the possibilities outside of the LEA. For in recent years four new categories of educational activity have arisen because of the inflexibility of the state's and LEAs' uniform educational provision. All appear to have developed despite, and in reaction to, the prevailing 'system'. Indeed most thrive outside it and are in danger of being seen as peripheral alternatives to it rather than integral parts of it. They can be summarised as follows:

- Small schools – particularly, but not exclusively, in rural areas.

- Schools for pupils who have been excluded by, or who have excluded themselves from, the large LEA school.

- New 'faith' schools.

- Networks of homeschoolers – a network of children who are educated at home by their parents because they are dissatisfied with the schools the LEA offers.

It is important to look at each category before drawing general conclusions.

1. Small rural schools

Small schools in rural areas are often the main, even the only, institution in a village with which people identify. Without the school, the village would become a mere dormitory for commuters to the nearest urban area. Yet the new world of teleconferencing and cottage industries may herald an awakening of rural life. For such people, who live and work in the village, a local school becomes essential. Otherwise, it is the young child who will have to commute unacceptably long distances.

However, the logic of the DfEE and LEA bureaucrat suggests that arcane economies of scale should hold sway. Village schools are small, often with less than a hundred pupils. So, they should be closed and the children sent long distances to larger schools, which has increasingly happened.

Quite apart from defending the virtue of the small school in its own right, an interesting alternative has arisen, as four schools in Dorset have demonstrated. Facing closure because they were 'too small', they banded together and formed four federal departments of one school. Each retained their own building's name, identity and special features. Instead of four separate headteachers, secretaries and so on, they now have one headteacher who herself commutes between them. She leads and inspires her staff, pupils and parents and has helped to preserve four key associations and assets in four thriving villages. It is possible to think of her as being a one person devolved LEA. This may be the way forward for other small rural schools which otherwise find difficulty realising the economies of scale.

2. Small urban schools for children whose needs are not answered by the LEA's large school

There is another kind of small school which has arisen not in rural but in inner-city areas. We have all now heard of 'Richard' who brought his school in Nottingham to a standstill and of the Ridings school in Yorkshire where several pupils held an entire school to ransom and made teaching impossible. Further, the more schools are asked to raise standards, the more we must expect them to want to expel that significant, but small, number of youngsters who do not fit into the large school setting. Many LEAs have special units or 'sin bins' for such youngsters. This may satisfy the large school's attitude of 'out of sight, out of mind', leaving them to get on with the task of educating the majority. But these centres in which the difficult pupil is placed generally have very low expectations and are not, in many cases, the solution even from the young person's or parents' point of view. The communities in which such young people create havoc are even less impressed.

St Paul's independent school in Birmingham's inner area of Balsall Heath became a GM school in September 1997 and is now an alternative which its large feeder LEA neighbouring schools value highly. The parents/guardians of its otherwise attention-seeking and disruptive pupils similarly value it. For in the small-school setting, they not only get the personal attention they hitherto lacked but, educationally and personally, they perform exceptionally well.

In one famous recent year these educational 'failures' came 6th from the top of Birmingham's GCSE league table of 70 secondary schools. There are now a number of similar ventures in other parts of the country, including Solihull whose enlightened LEA devised one from what had been an exclusion centre. As an exclusion centre, it would have failed its pending inspection. As a small school, it is beginning to work well.

As communities continue to unravel over the next few years, we must expect more pupils like Richard to arise. Until communities are strengthened, we must also assume that these pupils will get younger and younger. While most will be of secondary age, an increasing number will be of junior age. Unless we provide them with high quality, small urban schools suited to their special needs education before they acquire a permanently disruptive personality, we are storing up a very expensive future for ourselves and the communities in which such youngsters live.

3. Faith schools

Faith schools have been a feature of school life in this country since schooling began, with Anglican and Catholic as well as Jewish schools. However, a new breed of faith school has raised questions which are yet to be answered by the educational establishment. Some, like John Loughborough School in London's East End are Christian, catering mainly for youngsters of black parents, most of whom are Seventh Day Adventists. However, other parents anxious for their children's future, send them to the school because of its ethos and standards. It recently passed an Ofsted inspection with flying colours.

Many Muslim parents in the inner areas of our cities would, if they could, send their children to established faith schools. But not all can find such a place. Some now want their own Muslim school in exactly the same way that some Christian parents wish to send their children to a school with a

Christian ethos. A growing number of such Islamic schools have been founded as independent, charitable agencies by parents and teachers.

But, like St Paul's independent (now GM) school, such ventures struggle for the funds they need to balance their books. For parents from the inner areas cannot afford the kinds of fees which sustain their independent counterparts, such as Eton and Harrow. While one set of dissatisfied, but affluent, parents can exercise choice by buying their way out of the inadequate LEA school and sending them to fee-paying independent schools, the parents described here cannot. Their schools survive on jumble sales and dedicated teachers working for love rather than money. Like St Paul's, some of these schools are now seeking state, pupil-led, funding either by acquiring voluntary-aided or grant-maintained status. That is, these inner-area independent schools are seeking to opt *into* the state system of funding.

4. Education Otherwise networks

While education is compulsory for all to the age of 16, the 1944 Education Act had an escape clause titled 'Education Otherwise' which enables parents who choose to educate their children themselves to do so. Many thousands of parents who are dissatisfied with the education their LEA offers today take advantage of the clause and educate their child at home. These parents are not, as some have wrongly supposed, bearded seekers of an alternative haven. Most have taken a hard decision that, if one parent stays at home, he or she can do better for their child than any of the nearby schools. Such children achieve good results.

The experience of those who have chosen the 'Education Otherwise' means of educating their children is of considerable interest. For, of course, not every parent can teach their child all subjects, even though many have taught themselves an impressive array of disciplines in order to help their child. Some band together to employ one parent or a retired teacher of, say, maths, music or chemistry as required. Thus, children are taught both individually at home and together in networks which have arisen to cover specialisms. These networks begin to resemble a kind of detached or devolved school. Indeed what these parents say is that if only their local school were good enough, they would happily send their child to it. As it is not, then they are, in effect, forced to create a new one whose standards satisfy their aspirations. Mary Ann Rose who was a teacher, but who is educating her five children at home, plans with other parents to buy a small empty school building as a 'home-study centre'. Leslie Barson runs the Otherwise Club in London which caters for the special needs of 80 children who are educated both at home and at the club with the help of two peripatetic teachers.

Education Otherwise, the national organisation which parents have set up, estimates that the numbers of parents educating their children at home has doubled in the last five years to more than 20,000. This is the equivalent to 20 secondary schools or 40 primaries. The technology of education is, of course, becoming ever more sophisticated. Today, home-based parents can help their children by accessing the libraries of the world through their family television and personal computer, giving them the qualities needed to meet the challenges of the world of tomorrow. Thus there is the likelihood that more and more parents will see even good schools as being 'assembly-line' establishments when what their child needs to succeed in the adult world is 'just-in-time' learning in which home-based students access information as and when they need it.

Because this mode of education is still seen by the educational establishment as eccentric and not part of the state system, parents have great difficulty finding all the ingredients they need to educate their children in this way. For example, one might have thought that they could access the funds that their child would have accrued had he or she gone to a state school. But this has so far proved impossible. Education Otherwise parents get no financial assistance from the state. They have not only banded together to employ specialist assistance out of their own pocket, they are also exploring ways of paying costly GCSE and A-level exam fees by enrolling their children at one or more of the newly independent colleges. If this happens, there is the possibility that enterprising colleges will, in effect, become the sponsors or founders of devolved school networks in which pupils gather together for a limited period of time while doing most of their work at home – not unlike college and university students. Perhaps such a college or even a school could draw the money for students enrolled at it but taught in networks and schools elsewhere?

Once, the wealthy associations of Merchant Taylor's, Haberdashers and other businesses founded and managed schools. In future, colleges may be joined by modern captains of industry who already see the virtue in providing crèches and nurseries for their staff. It may be that they will be supported in such educational enterprises by the new suppliers of educational services to schools. For it must presently dawn on their research and development advisors that if they can supply teams of inspectors and other vital services to schools there is no reason why they should not also provide, support and develop schools as, for example, does the for-profit education company based in Manchester, Nord Anglia Education Plc. Indeed, there is no reason why an enterprising school or cluster of schools should not create its own mini-school, say, like St. Paul's, for those of their pupils who are found not to benefit from the large-school setting.

Just as we now look back in wonder at the days when the National Health Service once provided a standard set of spectacles so, on reflection, we may also begin to question the assumption that only the state's local authority is supposed to start and manage a school.

Thus, if we may call these 'Education Otherwise' networks schools, there are four kinds of school which have arisen alongside the previously monopolistic, 'one-size-fits-all' LEA system of schools which self-reliant, often materially poor, parents have built and now manage. They have expended this energy and effort because the choice they are offered by the 'system' is not, as they see it, good enough. Unlike the independent public schools which the dissatisfied affluent choose to maintain for their children, these schools are predominantly in inner areas whose parents are poor but no less choosy, ambitious and faithful for their children. This is a new and exciting phenomenon. The state's uniform 'system' is not just being challenged at the top of society, but also at the bottom, in a way which established thinking has yet to recognise or draw lessons from. What might those lessons be?

Choice, Diversity and Demand

It seems that the aspirations which parents have for their children and the aptitudes of children cannot be catered for within an old-style, uniform LEA school system. Pupils and parents are different and require different schools through which to grow and realise their talents and hopes. Where these schools do not exist or are under threat, they create or save and manage them.

The first part of this century saw the state intervene to create an educational system for all in place of one for the few. That was appropriate. But now that we have that system, people are at work improving upon and developing it. The enabling politician should not seek to conservatively restrain parents' hopes and enterprise or justify what was an appropriate standard for a past era, but facilitate and encourage these initiatives which herald a new one.

Although all four types of independent school have arisen separately as a result of parents' initiatives, there is no reason why these four categories of educational variety could not have been supported and funded in terms of the nationally agreed per capita formula we proposed above by central or local government. As the enterprising clothes shop manager might say to the customer who asks for a coat not held in stock at the time, 'Sorry sir, we do not have one. But we will make one up for you'. They call it 'Tailor made', the hallmark of care and distinction. In Europe – the Netherlands and Denmark for example – such schools are commonplace. Yet, in this country, because 'independent' schools are associated with privilege, few people have yet noticed that they could also, as is the case with St Paul's, benefit the underprivileged.

In an important article, Neil Reybekill (1997) points out that in Denmark local state schools (Folkeskole) exist happily alongside and on equal terms with independent schools (frie skoler). Indeed, all folkeskole 'must make provision for all the children resident in their skoledistrict, whether they attend their school or not'. Should the parents choose not to avail themselves of a place at that school, the funding follows the child to 'either another folkeskole or to a new independent school if parents band together to form one'. In Denmark, if you are unable to get a place in the state or private school of your choice then, 'as long as you can find 10 – 12 other parents who are in a similar position, you can start your own school. The government will help you to find premises, employ staff and run it'. Reybekill points out that because the same method of funding applies to state schools, private and new ones, 'it works as a unifying element'. Students can and do move freely in and out of the state sector and so do teachers.

It is surely time to see these four types of school not as alternatives or challenges to state education but as vital parts of a newly diverse and inclusive system of provision. They should be seen as a complement to existing educational provision which adds to the choices on offer to parents. For, today's parent-as-customer clearly requires a range of schools of different types to chose from to suit the different needs and aptitudes of their children. And, who better to devise them than teachers and parents together rather than some remote bureaucrat?

George Walden MP, former Minister of Higher Education under the Conservative government, had a similar idea but applied it to alternatives at the other end of the educational spectrum (Walden, 1996). Once the monopolistic state threatened the existence of the high-class direct grant schools, they quite understandably opted to become independent. Thus a whole tranche of ambitious and energetic parents were lost to the state system. Their time and effort was put into assuring that their child's newly independent school remained appropriate to their aspirations. Tempt those schools back into the state system, suggested Walden, and the parents of their children will again become a national asset rather than the vanguard of an élite and separate kind of schooling.

Thus in place of a division between a uniform state and, to either side of it, excluded independent alternatives, it is possible to envisage a burgeoning, all-inclusive system of state-funded but autonomous and self-governing schools which together spell choice and diversity. But choice and diversity are concepts which the educational establishment's egalitarian state monopoly recoiled from for a generation. While the customer's need for choice cannot be squared with the pyramid's principle of equality, it is enshrined in and legitimised by the model of the maypole and self-government.

Relevant to this discussion, Stephen Pollard, (Pollard, 1995), pointed out that

> 'We do, of course, have a fully functioning choice system in tertiary education. University "x" isn't made worse because University "y" is a good University – it is improved. Colleges play to each others strengths, and offer diverse courses and atmospheres. Choice in tertiary education has increased standards and access. It will do the same in primary and secondary education'.

Old Labour and the educational establishment are at one in having feared choice and, therefore, selection, because of its post-1944 association with the 11-plus exam which segregated children into just two types of school – grammar and secondary. Thus, for them, the uniform egalitarian comprehensive which replaced these two schools appeared to be the solution to a divisive conflict. But, this levelling-down and theoretically egalitarian solution failed in practice just as surely as the architect's off-the-peg municipal tower blocks which replaced the terraced houses of the Industrial Revolution. The outcome is that, today, tenants now vie with each other to press the switch which blow up the tower blocks before they are replaced with individually tailored new family housing, in the same way that parents avoid comprehensive schools and search for human, often small-scale, educational variety.

Howard Gardner first discussed the possibility that, as children are different, they might manifest several different kinds of intelligence or aptitude, rather than just exhibit either an academic or non-academic kind (Gardner 1993). He suggested that different people have different intellectual qualities for which different kinds of school are required. Like most things, if taken to over-simple extremes, selection and choice can be unhelpful. Simply because they took one form in the old grammar/secondary modern days, which resulted in a negative levelling-down reaction, there is no reason why they should not take a more positive form in the customer-oriented, multi-choice setting of today in which the academic bent is merely one of many which good schools might develop and businesses recruit. Thus, in place of levelling-down, we now need a combination of levelling upwards and sideways to cater for the plethora of distinct needs which no one school or cluster of schools can cater for. The sophisticated economy and society of tomorrow requires a variety of schools which complement each other in one diverse, many splendoured 'state system'.

Perhaps as Walden suggests, if those who have been wedded to the 1960s idea of 'uniformity and no choice' cannot quite bring themselves to admit their error, then such a phrase as 'choice by aptitude' might help them on their way.

In an old-style LEA of, say, 300 schools, it is possible to envisage the development of perhaps 30 clusters of 10 schools, each with nine primary and one secondary, each with its own cluster development plan, vision and ambitions for its pupils. Scattered amongst these, and in association with them, we could see here a faith school, there one for children with particular difficulties, and over there a newly integrated direct grant school. While retaining, as in Dorset, the distinct names and locations of these 300 schools, it is also possible to see one or more enterprising head in each of the 30 clusters becoming the driving force for distinction in one or more areas of educational excellence. Not one grammar school in each urban area so much as thirty clusters of excellent schools all playing to each other's strengths, all driven forward not by LEA officers but by a new breed of entrepreneurial headteacher and governor who are able to to train and support other, less visionary headteachers.

Does the LEA have a Function?

Those with a direct interest in the maintenance of the old-style LEA because they are employed by it, are in political control of it, or feel dependent upon it, make points and produce accounts which show why it should be retained. But should it? Is any aspect of the LEA's work left after the services and funds it supplies are devolved to schools and, through them, to independent suppliers? For, it is now the case that:

- Further and higher education have already left the LEA, and universities have always been self governing.

- In many authorities, adult education is already handled by another city department or independent colleges.

- The finance and management of schools is being phased from LEAs to the schools themselves. This money can and should be passed directly to them by means of a nationally agreed formula which leaves no one in any doubt as to what each school is entitled. This could be done by a computer based anywhere in the country.

- HMI Inspections are now overseen by Ofsted and are open to tender and competition. Similarly, the more regular inspections of schools at a local level can be bought in from independent educationalists by either schools or local authorities as required.

- Other independent agencies are offering quality support in every area of the curriculum. There are still gaps in the market of non-LEA suppliers but that is a direct consequence of the lingering LEA monopoly.

- The finance to fund or buy Education welfare officers and educational psychiatrists is easily and more effectively devolved to schools. Although the government rests the responsibility for these tasks in the hands of local authorities, they are, perhaps, better discharged by a Social Services Department than by an LEA.

- The finance for school meals, cleaning and caretaking can also most effectively be devolved out to schools or to neighbouring clusters of schools which will either provide these services themselves or buy them in from independent suppliers.

- The supply of temporary teaching staff and specialist peripatetic teachers is increasingly being provided by private sector agencies.

- The careers service has been subjected to competitive tender and is now delivered by a variety of different companies.

- Almost every non-educational specialist service, from payroll to legal advice, can be readily obtained on the High Street.

Decisions about the number of school places and the opening of new schools could be undertaken by a tiny LEA. But whether a whole city department is needed to discharge this function is doubtful. It seems that there is very little 'rowing' or service provision which the LEA has provided in the past, which, in future, cannot be offered more effectively by one or other of the following:

- Independent service suppliers.

- Schools themselves or clusters of schools.

- Other local authorities' departments or a quite new department.

Indeed, if LEAs were to vanish, the following is likely to result:

- All available funds for education would be targeted on schools and available for, or in support of, the classroom

- Management experience and maturity at the level of the school (head) and community (governors) would improve.

- Schools would become accountable not to remote bureaucrats but to the communities in which they are situated.

- The empire-building tendency of the LEA bureaucracy which has developed on the back of large budgets would end.

- Schools' attitude of dependence would change. They would independently and voluntarily see the point of, and deploy the means for, improving their performance and raising standards.

These are substantial gains. Even so, there are reasons of principle and practice which may suggest that an important new rôle for the LEA *or some local government equivalent* could be found. These reasons turn around the functions of 'steering' and enabling the new self-governing school to chart the right course and aim for high enough standards. So it is important to distinguish between the redundant old-style LEA and the visionary, steering, rôle of a new kind of authority.

As the principle of subsidiarity suggests, while all those things which can be devolved to schools or clusters or schools should be devolved, there are also vital things which arguably require an overarching body which stands between schools, remote Whitehall and the competitive market. To get them done, some agency is required which is accountable to local government. Shorn of the provision of almost all services, this remaining and inexpensive, but crucial, function includes the following components:

- As long as schools are funded from the public purse, they need to be held accountable to the taxpayer for the way those funds are spent. Therefore, first, local government will wish to assure itself that each school's accounts are, like those of other enterprises, audited annually. They will also wish to ensure that performance is monitored between formal Ofsted inspections to identify:

i) failing schools (to ensure that they close or improve);
ii) poor teachers and headteachers (to ensure that they are dismissed or improve);
iii) good schools (to ensure that good practice is disseminated);
iv) good teachers and headteachers (to ensure that their talents are emulated and deployed to maximum benefit).

Yet, while the local authority must be accountable for this monitoring it does not have to do it itself. Rather, as with the auditing of each school's budget, it must ensure that others who are well qualified perform the function. So, the local authority only needs to employ a very limited number of people who will ensure that:

- Others monitor the schools within its territory.

- Others take any subsequent action which that monitoring may require.

- Special needs also require a special monitoring rôle to ensure the highest standard, otherwise schools might lapse and particular kinds of pupil may lose out. Again, local authorities do not have to provide for special needs themselves, but they must ensure that someone does and that they do it very well.

- Applications to the DfEE, Europe and elsewhere for special funds and the allocation and monitoring of those funds is also a responsibility which the local authority might retain. Who the authority requires to discharge that responsibility is another question.

- Admissions also cannot be left to schools alone. Some pupils may not otherwise be catered for at all. However, who solves the problem for which the local authority is responsible is again open to question. Certainly, it need not be the local authority.

- Finally, just as each town and rural area needs its own personal identity, mayor and civic leader, so sets of schools and clusters of schools need their own regional vision. The new authority which we advocate may not be a manager, funder or controller, but it could be a creator of visions, an enabler as well as an inspector.

As with the national funding formula for schools, such a radical redrafting of the educational rôle of local government might be threatening to some. It would be wise to pilot it in a limited number of areas.

It is now commonly agreed that in a number of places like the London Borough of Hackney, one reason why schools have failed and parents are anxious is because they have been ill-served by their LEA. It really does not make sense to give a poor LEA the funds and support which schools need to deliver a first rate service in the classroom. It risks throwing good money after bad.

On the contrary, it would be more efficient to expect the local government to put the task out to tender. The bidders are likely to include:

- A successful school or a consortium of schools;

- A private supplier of educational services;

- The parents and community in which the schools are embedded.

The first such examples really choose themselves: Hackney and similar areas where the LEA has already conspicuously failed are the obvious contenders. Indeed, referring back to our earlier discussion, the proposal for the national funding formula could be piloted in the same areas as this tendering of LEA functions.

The government's White Paper (DfEE 1997) suggested that areas where schools are not achieving be declared Education Action Zones (EAZs). Little thought has been given to how such an EAZ might be managed. Applying the funding formula and contracting out in this way could be the way forward. Such a plan may not even need more funds. For, if the existing fraction of funds which the LEA retains to 'help' were offered to an independent bidder, it is likely that dramatic improvement would soon follow at no extra cost. Moreover, schools would also see what they had been missing – and what they could do – with the funds which the LEA had been squandering.

If the pilot areas are a success, then it would be possible, as with LM in the 1980s, to translate the first phase of a rolling programme which takes in increasing numbers of the nation's schools and local authority areas.

In 1946, Henry Morris said: 'Administration is only safe when it is in the hands of the philosopher and thinker, the teacher and the artist ... for whom administration exists merely as the instrument for realising quality and value' (quoted in Rée, 1973). Just as the new self-governing school needs the drive of a new entrepreneurial Head, so also the new enabling local authority needs a new kind of senior officer. Such a person will inspire schools within its region to greater heights by challenging them to assume the responsibility to improve upon their performance year on year – and then lets them get on with the task which only they can undertake, the delivery of high quality education to their children.

Neither this nor the other functions outlined above require the Town or County Hall local authority to work with a distinct and separate LEA. Indeed, some LEAs have experimented in imaginative new ways by forming a new Children's and Community Department which encompasses some features of the old Social Services and Education Departments.

The Funding of Local Authorities

Once we and, more to the point, each school knows exactly what its invisible budget should be from our suggested computer using a nationally agreed formula we can now turn to the distinct question: How should the new local authority be funded? Not, it should be clear, by asking it unfairly to top slice their budgets of schools. This exercise has been too open in the past to misinterpretation and, no doubt inadvertent, abuse. So a distinct and fresh means of funding the residual educational function of local authorities should be devised by the DfEE. For example, once the computer tells us what each school in an authority's area should and will receive, then an additional sum could be allocated to the authority of, say, two per cent of that amount. Repeat, this sum would not be deducted from the total schools' budget, but given to the local authority separately and in addition to it.

In an authority of 300 schools with 50 secondaries and 250 primaries, this would amount to £275 million.[1] Two per cent of this is £5.5 million, the equivalent of two and three-quarter secondary schools. If the future rôle of the local authority is not to build, control, manage, maintain and finance schools which are now self-governing but to challenge them to improve and, in partnership with Ofsted, ensure that their budgets and the quality of their work is audited, that seems to be an ample amount.

What is absolutely clear is that local authorities should not be expected to 'retain centrally' from schools what they need to carry out their new rôle. For the same misunderstandings and temptations which have arisen in the past would surely recur. Finally, as with schools, each local authority should be held accountable for the spending of its budget both financially and in terms of the quality of what it achieves with it, either by spending it on its own support staff or as the above pilot proposal suggests, on independent educational contractors.

---

[1] 50 x £2,000,000 + 250 x £700,000.

5 | New LEA, New Town Hall

The welfare state arguably was a great achievement and a substantial social advance upon the early days of the Industrial Revolution. Hunger, poverty, want and the need of every child for schooling had to be tackled. Yet, as the central and local government structures were constructed which provided unemployment, or income support and pension benefits, schools, houses and social care 'for' people, the welfare state came to erode people's sense of responsibility, initiative and ability to control the quality of their lives. It caused the local self-help associations through which people supported each other, found identity and pride to atrophy. The one-size-fits-all school and tower block created an unintended social desert which rendered life in urban neighbourhoods unsustainable.

It is difficult to accept that the very thing designed to dispense welfare, end ignorance and the other scourges of industrial society in fact contributed to a new kind of ignorance and poverty – weak and dependent people and communities. Yet, as pointed out in the opening quotations: give a hungry family fish, they will need more fish tomorrow and become dependent on the supplier. But, teach them how to fish and make fishing rods and you make them independent and proud.

The good school alone is not enough. The attitude and support of parents is, of course, pivotal. But, so too are all those friendly eyes, ears and voices of neighbours and local associations which can create a lively and compelling atmosphere. These are the 'little platoons' which are destined to become the cornerstone of the new welfare state. For, if properly resourced and supplemented, they are far more versatile, personally caring and adroit at delivering support and welfare than any externally imposed and institutionalised service. This implies a new compact between the people, their community and the community of communities, the city and the state.

The more self-reliant people and neighbourhoods become and the more the pyramids of both private and public institutions have been transformed into self-governing 'maypoles', the more voters have become alienated from politicians. While others have changed, the political process remains unreformed. Until recently it was unquestioningly supposed that the politically motivated councillor and MP should attempt to control central bureaucracies in order to supply uniform services to fractured and dependent neighbourhoods. Suited to the pyramids of the industrial world, the political party has become detached from the thrust of a better educated, better-informed, more confident citizen. Neither the representative politician nor the resident has yet been schooled in the needs of a post-industrial form of participatory democracy. Before the credibility gap between the politician and the public becomes unbridgeable, it is important to clarify new rôles.

It is not sufficient to devolve finances and managerial control to schools and other local caring, welfare delivering, agencies. Parts of the modern political process itself must also be devolved. Representative democracy only expects ordinary folk to exercise responsibility and make a choice once every five years. It expects them to leave the supply of services to Town Hall and Whitehall and to do nothing for themselves. To recapture the common sense of responsibility and ownership we need to add participatory democracy to the representative kind. Participatory democracy allows people to assume responsibility for key features of local life between elections. It allows them to act as school governors, become the directors of voluntary agencies and act like the good Samaritan to their neighbours. In a word, it calls for the rebuilding of sustainable communities, re-spinning the 'gossamer strands of memory' along which civilisation passes.

Old-style Town and County Hall departments cannot relate to, or easily facilitate, such participatory democracy. For they are organised in terms of specialist professional functions – education, social services, housing and so on, as well as in pyramid – like hierarchies. This suited the needs of large city-wide planning bureaucracies, but it is of little benefit to crumbling or resurgent neighbourhoods which recognise different boundaries and needs. One possibility is that a fresh, neighbourhood-sensitive, city department is now needed which cuts across the city's old bureaucratic specialisms and planning areas. This new department must regard neighbourhoods and the families, children and schools within them as the basic building blocks from which towns are constructed. Instead of being organised segmentally and hierarchically, this department should, therefore, subtend an array of geographically specific sub-departments, one for each neighbourhood or cluster of neighbourhoods. These neighbourhood sub-departments would marshall and deploy the levers of local government to enhance each area. It is not surprising, therefore, that many towns have developed neighbourhood offices in recent years and, with central government, have devised Single Regeneration Budgets, which cut across hierarchical departmental boundaries. While these developments have not always been in response to a clear neighbourhood voice, they are welcome signposts which point out the need to reinvent local government.

Because the aim of this new Children's and Community Department is to boost the capacity and confidence of the individual, see to it that others assist the developing child and take part in the revitalisation of neighbourhoods, it is sensible to devolve key parts of it out to area offices in each neighbourhood. Its offices would, in effect, become one-stop mini Town Halls. Again, it is possible to picture the proposed method of organisation in model form (see Figure 10).

The mini Town Hall would be the city's devolved top-down lever, with which co-ordinated bottom-up neighbourhood regeneration initiatives would liase. It might be based in an extension of one of each urban village's schools and become one of its focal features. These proposals are not idealistic. Hillingdon and Kent have merged several departments to create a new community-oriented one. Tower Hamlets has devolved most of its services. Braintree District Council has already implemented many of Osborne and Gaebler's suggestions.

In time, it is possible to see how the old pyramid-like Town Hall might be replaced with a sleek, visionary new centre, perhaps led by an elected mayor. But the radical reform of local government will not just happen. It must be prepared for by central government whose task it is to spell out the brand new rôle, point to good practice and encourage a new breed of 'philosopher and thinker, teacher and artist ... for whom administration exists merely as an instrument for realising quality and value'.

These reforms represent no more of an attack upon local government than John Harvey Jones' attempts to revitalise fading businesses by shifting them from pyramid-to-maypole-like structures signify an attack upon them. On the contrary, the proposed reforms could rescue the political process from decades of inertia and popular resentment and herald a new era of acceptance, appreciation and vigorous growth.

It is easy for defenders of the status quo to forget that the existing form of Town Hall and Whitehall democracy has already undergone many profound changes as people's requirements of it have matured. Just two centuries ago, Tom Paine and others fought for the 'rights of man'. In this century, women chained themselves to railings and staffed the munitions factories in the First World War to gain the vote. Full adult suffrage only came after the Second World War.

Democracy has evolved and must continue to keep pace with the times. Many of the reforms initiated in recent years could be improved and built upon rather than scrapped in a dated ideological attempt to return to the past. The array of quangos and trusts have been rightly criticised as unaccountable to their local communities. But, reconceived to embed them in the area they serve, with clear lines of accountability and clear rights of participation for local communities, new self-governing agencies have the potential to be much more responsive and entrepreneurial, than the monopolies of local government they replace.

Some who wish to preserve the status quo of representative democracy will say: 'People are not ready for it and they are never likely to become competent to exercise such responsibilities'. This is the age-old argument of those who wish to retard the inclusion of excluded voters/participants. White South Africans argued it to exclude Nelson Mandela and black South Africans. Property owners in this country argued it against non-property owners, men against women. The argument is no more valid now than it ever was.

Others will argue: 'People will not respond, they are apathetic, we already struggle to fill existing positions of responsibility without opening up new ones'. Perhaps, if what is on offer is more tokenism, not genuine participation but consultation after decisions have been made by elected

Figure 10: The new Town Hall structure

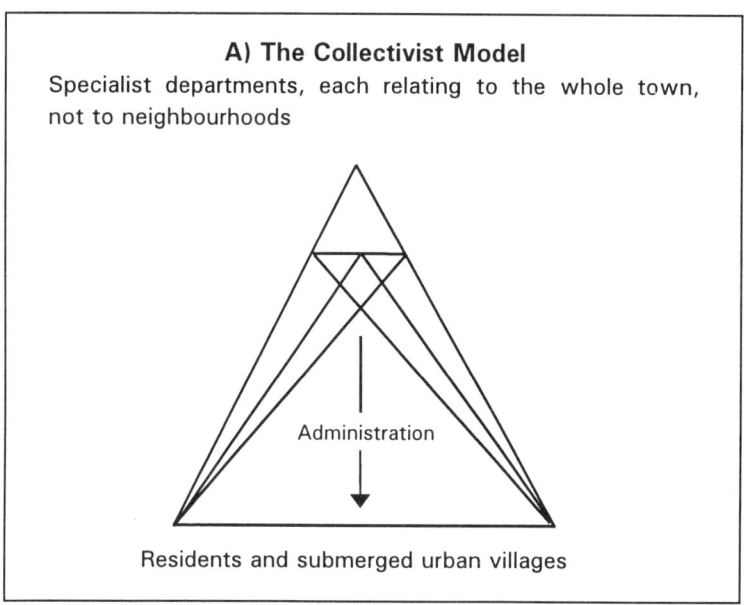

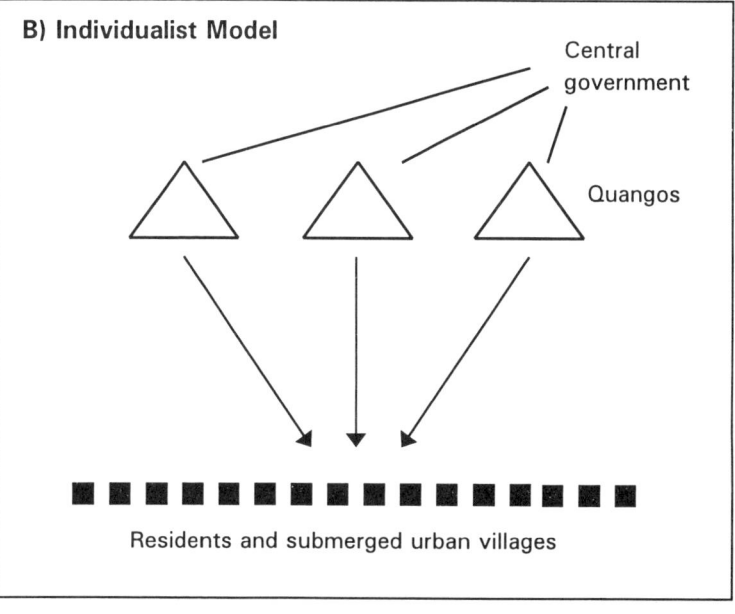

Figure 10: (Continued)

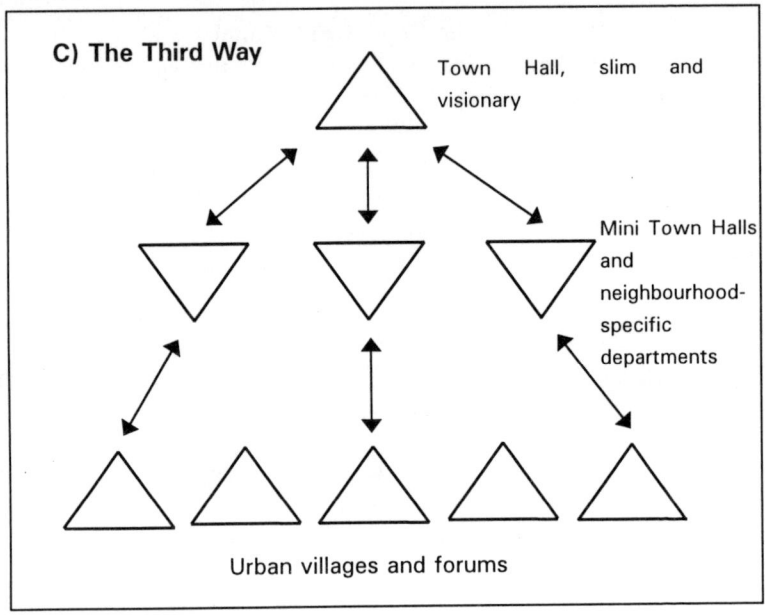

representatives. But, give local communities real assets to develop their interests and build their neighbourhood afresh and they will do so, as for example in the town hall system in many towns and villages in New England where townspeople vote on annual education budgets, make decisions on key policies, etc. No doubt a little encouragement will help after years of neglect and of experts telling amateurs that they will only make mistakes while themselves building structures which later have to be dismantled after having harmed a generation. That is why the rôle of self-governing schools, their family and enterprise centres and independent colleges is so important. They can aid, inform, educate and give ordinary people the extraordinary confidence that will empower them to make a real difference to the substance and quality of their lives.

As Charles Leadbetter wrote in *The Rise of the Social Entrepreneur*:

> 'We need to commit ourselves to a wave of social innovation, lasting years, to create new welfare services and new organisations to deliver them. We need both new ideas and

policies, as well as institutions to deliver them. We need a new generation of welfare institutions which are voluntaristic, open and flexible yet professional, innovative and business like. To create a new social welfare system we need a new breed of social entrepreneur. Britain has a long history of welfare innovation. At the time of its creation the welfare state was the culmination of this great reforming tradition. Yet one of the greatest costs of the welfare state has been its crowding out of organisations capable of producing welfare reform. We need to return to this voluntaristic tradition of welfare innovation. Social welfare has never been solely the province of the state.' (Leadbetter, 1997, p. 26).

6 | Conclusion and Recommendations

There are times when established ways of thinking and working are washed away and new attitudes surge to the fore. Many accept that this is true of the welfare state's system of social security benefits and pensions which are now so costly, have unintentionally institutionalised the value of care and made people dependent. Yet, communal bonds and associations of mutual support have subsequently unravelled to such an extent, and educational standards are so worryingly inadequate, that it is also time to think the previously unthinkable in all features of the welfare state.

The Butskellite consensus between the post-war parties about the benefits of the welfare state's Town and County Hall LEA monopoly of education, held right through the 1960s and 1970s. During that time Secretaries of State for Education Shirley Williams and Margaret Thatcher vied with their predecessor, Tony Crosland, to close 'every last (expletive deleted) grammar school' and impose uniform comprehensives which were financed and managed by, and thus dependent on, large bureaucracies.

It is to the Conservative government's credit that in the 1980s it began a series of reforms which were designed to raise standards in all schools and for all pupils. With the benefit of hindsight, we can now see that it was not sufficient to lead schools to these reforms – Ofsted inspections, league tables, SATs and so on. Rather, the prevailing educational culture which taught schools to be dependent on LEAs needed to be radically altered before they would become self-motivating, and voluntarily accept responsibility.

Unfortunately, the government's attempt to alter the educational culture by reforming the way schools were managed was itself flawed and divisive. In particular, it was assumed that all schools would leap at the chance to become GM and independent – whereas their dependence on the existing system was fostered by LEAs who, in turn, could not envisage how they might invent for themselves a new, enabling, rôle. The outcome? Further confusion, which today allows old Labour to argue without even the hint of a deprecating smile that it is essential to return to the drab pre-1980s days of overbearing Town and County Halls.

This is not an alternative. It is possible to accept the need for radical reform, go beyond the division of GM versus LM, and put in place confident, self-governing schools and clusters of schools which will happily enter into a productive new partnership with redrafted, visionary and slimmed-down local authorities.

Making the existing welfare state's way of facilitating and managing education move from the industrial era's collectivist 'pyramid' to the modern devolved 'maypole' enables the funding and organisation of schools to benefit in 10 significant ways:

1. There is more money already in the system than we supposed. Schools do not so much need *new* money as to access that which is already in the system. It is important to clarify just how much money is available (with the help of independent auditors, rather than the partial LEA), then allocate those funds to schools where they are most needed and not to the old LEA supplier.

2. Standards will not necessarily rise if more money is put into the system, for, a) it is not likely to reach the classroom without radical change and, b) attitudes in the classroom must change so that existing money is used to maximum benefit.

3. Schools of all kinds should be made self governing. It is no longer relevant for them to be managed or funded by bureaucrats. They may well find the task of assuming responsibility for raising standards more exciting and rewarding if they are encouraged to cluster together to find mutual support and confidence. Indeed, this may be the only way that their budget can be put to most effective use, thus enabling them to provide home-grown, specially targeted, services.

4. New, independent suppliers of educational services will also flourish alongside schools in this situation and provide them with a quality product which is superior to that

offered by the old LEA. They are not market-driven enemies of schools, but cherished and cost-effective high quality friends which can invest in and produce innovative research and development of a higher calibre than the LEA once offered.

5. To make the best use of these services, their budgets and autonomy, governors need to be vigorous; headteachers need to be enterprising and to have to hand a new breed of school-based administrator and other non-teaching helpers.

6. In place of the old LEA, *at most* what is needed are new local authority departments led by enablers not administrators, and which, *at most* 'steer' rather than 'row', set targets and hold schools to public account for the quality of their performance. These departments should be responsible for stimulating the regeneration of urban communities as well as educational excellence so that schools can operate in catchment communities which support rather than undermine them.

7. Because each school can be funded by a computer working to a nationally agreed per capita formula there is a need to fund the redrafted local authority separately so that it is not dependant on taking money which should go to schools.

8. Many schools would respond by both raising standards and playing a key rôle in the rebuilding of the communities their pupils live in by opening Family Centres, Home/School Study and Education Enterprise Centres, thus enabling local people to gain pride and ownership over the education process. Schools – buildings, grounds and staff – are vital assets which can be owned by local people and seen as part of the texture of the neighbourhood in which they are located. Thus schools can become the engine which drives the 'little platoons' through which real welfare is delivered in neighbourhoods at a personal level.

9. Independent educational initiatives should be allowed to flourish, not outside or as alternatives to the 'state' system but, as in Europe and America, as part of a diverse state-funded system.

10. Finally, as New Labour seeks to dot the 'i's and cross the 't's of its new policies it must also check that its values are appropriate to the modern age. The egalitarianism of the past implied levelling down, making individuals and variety fit into a uniform pattern. On the contrary, we must not pull the best down, but challenge them to help the weaker and less successful to catch up. In place of making people and agencies dependent upon state provision, we must help them to be free and independent. That is, we must expect people to exercise the responsibility to choose and create diverse experiences suited to their uniquely different aptitudes. In place of a divided system, in which 20 per cent succeeded and 80 per cent failed, this offered some hope. But today's world requires that all succeed, develop and apply their different talents in different ways. This spells diversity – choice by aptitude and returning to people and local educational establishments the responsibility and pride which comes from ownership. That is as different from the simple selection which divided people into grammar and secondary school pupils as is chalk from cheese. So New Labour needs new attitudes, new values and a new language if it is to succeed in transforming educational achievements and rebuilding sustainable communities.

It can be done. But, change, any change, can be frightening and could cause a defensive reaction. So, after many years of confusion and uncertainty, it is sensible to first pilot the developments advocated here in a limited number of sympathetic authorities and eager schools before attempting to apply them nationwide. Thus, all, even the most anxious, could see the practical benefits and that reform is heading in a positive and clearly defined direction.

Perhaps, therefore, the DfEE could follow CfBT's example, fund an initial tranche of cluster facilitators and enable a few enlightened authorities to pass on all available funds to schools while developing new Children's and Communities' Departments.

If a failing school can be turned around by an enterprising, clear-sighted head in three years, then it is surely possible to turn round cumbersome and failing local authorities and the nation's schools within ten years. Communities may take a little longer, even with the help of Family and Educational Enterprise Centres.

That is the challenge – to re-engineer the way ignorance can be banished and real welfare delivered.

Appendix

How is it possible that assumed knowledge about the amount of education funds which could go to schools is retained by LEAs is wrong and that there is far more money available to schools than we had supposed? Nick Seaton points out that the LEAs take two sums away from schools before they retain the 5 to 15 per cent of the budget which we actually know about. His calculations can be pictured as follows:

CURRENT METHOD OF ALLOCATION OF FUNDS TO LEA SCHOOLS

Standard Spending Assessment (SSA)
(Government grant for all local services, excluding police)

General School Budget
(amount allocated by Local Authority for its own services and schools)

minus 'Mandatory Exceptions'
(capital expenditure, financing, special needs etc. – decided by LEA)

minus 'Discretionary exceptions not subject to limit'
(home to school transport, school meals etc. – decided by the LEA)

= Potential schools Budget (PSB)

minus 'Discretionary exceptions subject to limit'
(advisory services etc. : limited to a maximum of 15% of the PSB)

= Aggregated Schools Budget (ASB)
(i.e. the amount to be divided between the schools in the LEA)

Seaton shows what this means for Gloucestershire, which has constantly claimed that it could not fund its schools because of central government cuts:

ALLOCATION OF FUNDS BY GLOUCESTERSHIRE LEA (1995–96)

GSB   £112 million   100%
subtract mandatory Exceptions   £18 million   16.1%
subtract Discretionary Exceptions
(not subject to limit)   £6 million   5.4%

PSB   £88 million   78.6%
subtract Discretionary exceptions
(subject to limit)   £8 million   7.1%

ASB   £80 million   71.4%

Seaton then lists 5 other authorities:

ALLOCATION OF FUNDS BY OTHER LEAs (1995-96)				
	GSB	ASB	ASB as % of GSB	Retention by LEA
Surrey	£272 miln	£185 miln	68%	32%
Derbyshire	£292 miln	£201 miln	69%	31%
Shropshire	£136 miln	£94 miln	69%	31%
Cambridge-shire	£196 miln	£137 miln	70%	30%
Birmingham	£398 miln	£283 miln	71%	29%

If the figures are correct, their implications are staggering. So, we must ask: how is it that nobody else has spotted the enormous potential for raising standards and increasing diversity by using existing funds differently?

Seaton's figures have been initially checked by independent management consultants. In a report to the CfBT, they write that: 'His main point about the arcane nature of LMS accounting is spot on.' They observe that the 'level of ignorance and naivety about these issues ... is frankly breathtaking. No-one in Councils (or Government) has gone out of their way to displace this ignorance; quite the opposite.' For, of course, it is in the embattled LEA's interest as a product that nobody should notice the financial advantage to it or the disadvantage to school and pupil as consumer.

It follows that by devolving so little, LEAs have 'effectively prevented a mixed economy of service provision from developing. Schools have had little purchasing power and the associated opportunities have never been opened up to other providers'. So the clustering of schools and their ability to purchase from the independent suppliers has been inhibited. As the consultants conclude: 'The current basis of calculation has had the direct result that a genuine market has not developed for services to schools. Only in a small minority of cases (such as Kent, Essex, Norfolk, Solihull) have services been genuinely market tested.' In this sense, 'there has been a grudging and reactionary response to LMS; schools' naivety has simply colluded with reactionary producer interest in most cases'.

Thus, it is possible to argue that 'Conservative policies, paradoxically, have not developed a market-led approach to education services'. Rather, the 'current basis of calculation has perpetuated ... (the) dependency culture in schools (especially primary schools) ... Were schools and their governors to be made fully and openly aware of [this] ... there would be massive pressure...' to change the way existing finance is distributed.

References/Bibliography

Abbott J. (1994): *Learning Makes Sense*, Letchworth: Education 2000.

Atkinson, D. (1994): *The Common Sense of Community*, London: DEMOS.

Atkinson, D. (1994): *Radical Urban Solutions*, London: Cassell.

Campbell, J., Halpin, D. and Neill, S. (1996): 'Primary Schools and Opting Out: Some Policy Implications', *British Journal of Educational Studies*, Vol. 44, pp. 248-249.

Department for Education and Employment (DfEE) (1997): Excellence in Schools, London: HMSO.

Field F. (1995): *Making Welfare Work*, London: Institute of Community Studies.

Field, F. (1996): *Stakeholder Welfare*, London: The Institute of Economic Affairs.

Fitz, J., Halpin, D. and Powers, S. (1993): *Grant Maintained Schools: Education in the Market Place*, London: Kogan Page.

Goleman, D. (1996): *Emotional Intelligence*, London: Bloomsbury.

Gardner H. (1993): *Multiple Intelligences*, New York: Basic Books.

Hanushek, E. (1996): 'Measuring Investment in Education', *The Journal of Economics Perspectives*, Fall, pp. 9-30.

Handy, C. (1989): *The Age of Unreason*, London: Hutchinson.

Hargreaves, D. (1994): *The Mosaic of Learning*, London: DEMOS.

Hargreaves D. (1997): 'A Road to the Learning Society', *School Leadership and Management*, Vol. 17, No. 1, pp. 9-21.

Leadbetter, C. (1997): *The Rise of the Social Entrepreneur*, London: DEMOS.

Lunt, I., Evans, J., Norwich, B. & Wedell, K. (1994): *Working Together*, London: David Fulton.

Meighan, R. (1997): *The Next Learning System*, Nottingham: Education Heretics Press.

Osborne, D. & Gaeble, E. (1993): *Reinventing Government*, New York: Plume.

Phillips, M. (1996): *All Must Have Prizes*, London: Little Brown.

Pollard, S. (1995): *Schools, Selection and the Left*, London: The Social Market Foundation.

Rée, H. (1973): *Education Extraordinary*, London: Peter Owen.

Reybekill, N. (1997): 'Vouchers, Inclusion and the Limits of Freedom', *Forum*, Vol. 39, No. 2.

Rifkin, J. (1995): *The End of Work*, New York: Tardew Putnam.

Sachs, J. (1997): *The Politics of Hope*, London: Jonathan Cape.

Schumacher, E. (1974): *Small is Beautiful*, London: Abacus.

Seaton, N. (1996): *School Funding*, London: The Centre for Policy Studies.

Smith, D.J. & Tomlinson, S. (1989): *The School Effect*, London: Policy Studies Institute.

Tooley, J. (1996): *Education Without the State*, London: Institute of Economic Affairs.

Walden, G. (1996): *We Should Know Better: Solving the Education Crisis*, London: Fourth Estate.

Wilson, J.Q. (1993): *The Moral Sense*, New York: Free Press.

The Debate on Higher Education

Challenging the Assumptions

Higher education in the UK is at a crucial juncture in its history. Its funding is in crisis, and morale amongst students and academics perilously low. This monograph offers two contributions to the debate.

Like many of the nationalised industries of old, producer-driven higher education suffers from inefficiencies and lack of responsiveness to its consumers: Adrian Seville shows how modularisation – the introduction of 'quasi'-markets in higher education – could ameliorate some of these problems.

His paper explores fundamental issues, and challenges whether the current quality control mechanisms in higher education can be considered satisfactory even in a traditional university setting, let alone when modularisation is introduced.

Tooley's contribution takes the debate a step further. The suggestion of 'quasi'-markets in higher education begs the question as to why not 'genuine' markets? Hence he examines the fundamental assumption which remains unchallenged in much of the current debate: why should government be involved in higher education at all? He looks at the major justifications given for government intervention, and finds each wanting.

Government is not needed to make higher education opportunities available. Indeed, there are negative effects of such intervention, including qualification inflation. Finally, the desirable goal of equity in terms of access to higher learning only needs the minimal intervention of private income-contingent loans for tuition and maintenance, not the gamut of interference with which we are familiar.

The Institute of Economic Affairs
2 Lord North Street, Westminster, London SW1P 3LB
Telephone: 0171 799 3745 Facsimile: 0171 799 2137
E-mail: iea@iea.org.uk Internet: http://www.iea.org.uk

£10.00

ISBN 0-255 36409-1